CW00420364

ENTREPRENEURIAL SALES

The practical guide to being
a more entrepreneurial, sales-savvy
small business owner

by Paul Durrant FISM

"I believe that every small business owner needs to be more innovative, disruptive and sales-focused in todays' ultra-competitive marketplace"

Paul Durrant

Printed by Amazon: Please visit your regional Amazon
website to obtain further copies of this book.

ISBN: 978-1-9162304-0-8

Copy editing: ACB Proofreading – www.acbproofreading.com
Design & typesetting: David Siddall Multimedia – www.davidsiddall.com

Contents

INTRODUCTION

My name is Paul Durrant and I am delighted to bring you this book, which is a distillation of my 30 years' experience in sales, combined with my observations of working with some very successful entrepreneurs and seasoned sales professionals.

During my relatively long career in sales, I have held a number of different roles, including tele-sales, account management, field sales, business development, national sales and sales management – all of which have vastly contributed towards my learning and development.

In addition, I have sold to virtually every type of consumer and business type and worked in many different industries including retail, fire protection, media sales, office products, courier sales, vehicle rental sales and records management.

Using this accumulated wealth of sales and business experience, I now help small business owners, sales leaders and salespeople to sell better and sell more.

What I have also concluded over this time is that not all business owners have the same levels of entrepreneurship and that not all salespeople have the same natural selling instincts – so why is this?

Are we born or made?

Psychologists and theorists have long speculated as to whether entrepreneurs are born or made. In other words, are very successful business owners born with their entrepreneurial gifts or do external factors such as environment and timing play a significant part in their make-up?

There have been many studies attempting to answer this entrepreneurial nature v. nurture question, and the collective evidence is, unfortunately, rather inconclusive.

What many of the aforementioned entrepreneur studies do indicate (especially the studies which looked at twins with shared DNA but different upbringings) is that whilst your genetics can play a part in actually starting a business in the first place, they play no real part in your business being ultimately successful!

> *"The secret of getting ahead is to get started."*
> *(Mark Twain)*

The exact same question is often asked about top performing salespeople, i.e. are they born or made? In an article written by Steve W. Martin (Sales Linguistics Expert) for the Harvard Business Review, his research concluded that:

- 70% of top salespeople are born with 'natural' instincts which play a critical role in determining their sales success
- Fewer than 30% of top salespeople are self-made (they 'make' their own success)
- 40% of people who enter sales will fail or quit
- 40% are only average performers
- 20% are above-average performers (in line with Pareto's 80:20 Principle)

NB. These figures do vary according to industry and the complexity of the sale.

The above research suggests that the overwhelming majority of top-performing salespeople are gifted. However, near enough a third are self-made successes who have risen to the top of their profession, through their own endeavours.

This means that for those that are unenlightened (when it comes to the art of sales), you can learn to talk the talk, even if you haven't been born with the 'gift of the gab'!

Being successful in business

To survive in business (let alone be successful), a small business owner needs to have an entrepreneurial outlook, a viable concept and business model, and also be at the very least competent in sales – because sales is the lifeblood of any business.

A viable business model combines strategy, goals, customers and monetising products and services into profit. To make a profit, you need to make a sale and this is how virtually all businesses generate revenue, cashflow and profit – which can then, of course, be reinvested back into the business to further innovate and grow.

Even charities need to be sales-focused in order to promote their cause and compete with all the other charitable organisations out there – in what is now a very competitive 'giving' sector.

Most commercial business models are based on developing a product or service that meets the needs or wants of a particular target market or markets. That particular business will then engage with their target market, identify sufficient numbers of sales (prospective customer) leads, nurture those leads and then convert as many as possible into paying customers, i.e. generate SALES!

Sales is not a dirty word

There are a lot of misconceptions about sales, with the biggest one being that sales is in some way manipulative and dishonest.

There are, of course, some 'sharp' sales practitioners out there but you will always unfortunately get unscrupulous operators in any type of profession – including sales (yes, sales is a profession)!

> *"Selling is not a pushy, winner-takes-all, macho act. It is an empathy-led, process-driven, and knowledge-intensive discipline. Because, in the end, people buy from people."*
> *(Subroto Bagchi – Co-founder of Mindtree)*

There are professional institutes and associations for the sales industry and most of these work to a code of ethics or standards. I belong to the ISM (Institute of Sales Management), which has its code of professional conduct, and there are other sales industry bodies out there that require their membership to behave ethically.

You can also get professional qualifications in sales and marketing, e.g. the ISM offers a Level 6 qualification (equivalent to a full bachelor's degree), aimed at senior sales managers, directors or those aspiring to progress to a senior sales level.

Given the importance of sales, it is surprising how many business owners do not even see themselves as being in sales and purposely shy away from the 'S' word; as mentioned above, they see it as something that is odious, disdainful or even dishonourable, i.e. something they don't want to associate themselves with. Unfortunately, this blinkered approach will ultimately be detrimental to their business!

Equipping yourself for business success

Business owners today have to have a wide variety of skills and at least a basic understanding of each of the key primary business functions, which are:

- Administration
- Operations
- Finance
- Sales and marketing
- IT (Information Technology)
- HR (Human Resources)

Some of these functions can be outsourced but this may not be possible in the early stages of starting up your business venture.

Success in business is also about making the most of any opportunity that comes your way, whether that be winning a new deal, collaborating with a new strategic partner or exploiting a new market opportunity.

Business is full of opportunities but being ready and prepared to take full advantage of those inevitable 'profit making' opportunities that present themselves is what successful business ownership is all about.

How 'sales-savvy' are you?

Launching a new business venture is one of the biggest challenges there is and if you were to ask a room full of aspiring or start-up small business owners what their biggest business challenge might be, then many would probably say 'generating enough sales – consistently'.

Indeed, a past government report produced by Lord Young found that 'lack of sales' was one of the major factors that contributed to why only about 50 per cent of UK small businesses make it to year five.

This high mortality rate sadly continues to rise to about 70 per cent by year ten!

The even sadder thing is that this statistic is no real great surprise given that most business owners do not have a sales background or any formal sales training, yet are typically doing the selling (especially in the early years). This means that three quarters of all small business owners are lacking any real 'savvy' when it comes to sales!

There is a long-established saying that goes 'you don't know what you don't know' – so if you are deficient in the 'sales experience and know-how' department, then that is clearly no fault of your own.

What you could be held accountable for was is if you did nothing about addressing your sales deficiencies, because having a better understanding of what sales is all about will ultimately profit both you and your own business!

> *"Knowledge born from actual experience is the answer to why one profits; lack of it is the reason one loses."*
> *(Gerald M. Loeb)*

Do you need some help?

The report referred to in the last section goes on to conclude that many small business owners do not seek the external expert help that they need at key stages of their development. They may, indeed, have a recognition that they need help but typically do not summon the will to seek out that all-important help.

This failure to engage with external expert help is, in my experience, down to a number of motivational factors:

- Denial
- Pride
- Cost Implication
- Apathy

Firstly, being in a state of denial is probably the most common of these factors and psychologists have identified denial as being the primary defence or coping mechanism which many people use to cope with really stressful situations.

Denial involves masking external events from our conscious awareness and allows us to pretend that a particular problem isn't real, but this approach doesn't address the problem to hand.

Being open to others' independent and impartial views and keeping yourself grounded by accepting that you cannot be an expert in everything will allow you to counter your limiting and damaging state of denial.

Second, pride can be a factor when a small business owner simply does not want to accept that they have failed in any way and that they may need help. I see this mostly with male mid-life business owners who see their business as 'their baby' and therefore act very protectively towards it. Again, this is a very damaging stance but can be countered by firstly recognising and then addressing your foibles and fallibilities.

Third, cost implication is another common factor. Getting external expert help can come with the assumption that the cost associated with that help will be high. There is, of course, a cost attached to anything, but what would be the long-term cost of not addressing a problem that could ultimately result in your business failing?

Researching and testing the market for any professional help should allow you to arrive at a fair price for the help that you need; always weigh up your ROI (Return On Investment) against your initial upfront cost of help to help you come to a more informed decision.

Finally, apathy is another common factor, which can be down to a small business owner just not recognising the severity of their problem or feeling that there just isn't enough time in the working day to address their problem.

In some cases, apathy can be the manifestation of anxiety and if you are really anxious about something, then this can lessen your capacity to deal with a problem.

Apathy, in this context, can be caused by a number of things, including fatigue, low levels of serotonin (often referred to as the feel-good chemical), having a negative mindset (that has become entrenched over a prolonged period of unhappiness) and lack of enjoyment, i.e. not having enough pleasurable distractions in your life.

NB. I will be talking about mindsets in more detail later in this book.

A combined mind and body approach is therefore needed here to counter any apathetic feelings that you may have. Spending time with friends, enjoying leisure pursuits, taking time away from your business, keeping a busy productive schedule and exercising regularly will help you feel much less apathetic about ultimately resolving your business-related problems.

> *"Willpower is the key to success. Successful people strive no matter what they feel by applying their will to overcome apathy, doubt or fear."*
> (Dan Millman)

How this book can help you

If you are an existing business owner or an aspiring business owner, e.g. a salesperson looking to start your first business, then discover in this book how to:

- Develop an entrepreneurial mindset
- Broaden your sales skills
- Toughen your mental resolve
- Grow your sales and your business

This book is designed as a 'pick-up, put-down' reference guide (rather than a detailed personal biography) and will show you how take advantage of any opportunity that comes your way i.e. become an accomplished entrepreneurial seller.

Image by Gerd Altmann from Pixabay

Additional 'Entrepreneurial Sales' training

To accompany this book, I have developed an online 'Entrepreneurial Sales' training course, which consists of ten different modules and five downloadable sales tools to use and keep.

Please us the promo code 'EPSALES' to get a 20% discount off this additional training resource. You can view this course and ten more sales training courses on the PDT Sales Academy page at: *https://pdtsalesconsultancy.co.uk/sales-training/*

1. WHAT IS ENTREPRENEURIAL SALES?

So, what does the term 'Entrepreneurial Sales' actually mean? In essence, it's my term for how an aspiring or existing small business owner can adopt a far more innovative, disruptive and sales-focused mindset, which will then help them grow and scale their business faster, i.e. become an entrepreneurial seller.

Before I go into more detail about entrepreneurial sales and becoming an entrepreneurial seller, I first need to define what an archetypal entrepreneur is and how being entrepreneurial doesn't automatically mean that you are sales-savvy!

What is an entrepreneur?

The standard dictionary definition for an entrepreneur is:

> *'A person who sets up a business or businesses,*
> *taking on financial risks in the hope of profit'*

... whilst the lengthier business directory definition is:

> *'Someone who exercises initiative by organising a venture to take benefit of an*
> *opportunity and, as the decision maker, decides what, how, and how much of a*
> *good or service will be produced'*

In other words, an entrepreneur is risk-taking, forward-thinking and opportunistic because they have been courageous enough to start up their own business in the first place.

It takes a lot of courage to start up a new business venture and be master of your own destiny. It also requires a certain amount of vision to 'think outside the box', i.e. see a commercial opportunity where others don't and then take a leap of faith.

I have been fortunate enough over the years to work with (and be mentored by) several successful entrepreneurs who took that 'leap', and the description of an entrepreneur above, in my experience, is a representative and accurate description.

How entrepreneurial a business owner is depends on the level of risk they have taken and how accepting they are that their project could completely fail. The true 'serial' or 'seasoned' entrepreneurs are the ones that are prepared to take more than one leap, accept failure as a likely outcome, learn from any resulting mistakes and then go again, until they ultimately find the right successful formula!

They then repeat this process in other (sometimes unrelated) markets, to build up a diverse portfolio of business interests, projects and businesses. The entrepreneur's formula seems to be:

| 1. Launch | 2. Fail | 3. Pivot | 4. Repeat |

... until a successful and viable business model (or models) is achieved.

Many entrepreneurs that I have seen up close and worked with seem to have common inherent qualities. Numerous studies have shown that serial entrepreneurs display noble qualities such as social responsibility and wealth creation for others, but in my experience the seven most common entrepreneurial traits are:

1. **Innovation** (having a dynamic 'game-changing' idea or concept)
2. **Vision** (a clear idea of the endgame for their business)
3. **Passion** (a real conviction about their business ideas and concepts)
4. **Strategy** (seeing the bigger picture and where the opportunities lie)
5. **Drive** (the courage and energy to execute their business ideas)
6. **Resilience** (the ability to overcome setbacks and adversity)
7. **Leadership** (the ability to engage and inspire others along their journey)

The 'sales-savvy' small business owner

Being an entrepreneurial small business owner who is just as 'sales-savvy' – i.e. they have previous sales experience and/or a good level of sales acumen – isn't a given.

Any small business owner may have a great idea or be extremely talented in what they do and have taken a number of risks in starting up their business venture, but getting their idea to market and converting a sufficient number of sales leads into actual paying customers is altogether another matter.

In my experience, only about a quarter of business owners have a practical sales background or have had any formal sales training, therefore selling does not come naturally to them. In fact, many do not see themselves as being in sales at all!

Some inexperienced sellers will take to sales more readily than others and reveal a naturally inbuilt talent for selling. They are typically able to carry the burden of a sales target as lightly as they carry themselves.

Others will struggle under the expectation of only being as good as last month's figures, whilst constantly having to be on top of their selling game.

Is there a competent salesperson inside you?

Just as entrepreneurs are associated with being creative, innovate risk-takers (but some fit that mould much more than others), salespeople are often seen as being self-centred, manipulative and untrustworthy (especially here in the UK).

This is not the case in the USA though, where sales is rightly seen as a profession and from where much of modern sales innovation and best practice originates.

So, the question is, are good salespeople born or made too?

Sales is 50% confidence and 50% competence

Being competent in something obviously plays a big part in what end results you achieve, but confidence also plays a big part – especially in sales.

If you think about it, most of us are normally put off buying something from someone who might appear unconfident or unsure about themselves, what they are selling or both. In other words, confidence will normally sway our buying decision.

Knowledge is also important when it comes to selling, but so is enthusiasm.

> *"Confidence and enthusiasm are the greatest sales producers in any kind of economy."* (O.B. Smith)

How should a buyer be expected to get enthusiastic about something if the seller is unenthusiastic or patently less knowledgeable about their own offering than you are?

Conversely, we don't buy from over-confident salespeople, i.e. someone who comes across as being arrogant, either, but we do expect a salesperson to have a competent level of confidence, i.e. act like they know what they are talking about.

I have noticed over a long career in sales that spans 30 years that proficient and top-performing salespeople normally display the necessary levels of confidence and competence, as well as these additional traits or attributes:

1. **Self-assured** (they are comfortable in their own skins and in what they sell)
2. **Knowledgeable** (about their customer, their market, their competition and their product/service offering)
3. **Insightful** (they use their superior micro and macro-market knowledge to influence the thinking of buyers)
4. **Driven** (they are competitive, hungry and disciplined in all that they do)
5. **Strategic** (they plan ahead to get ahead – with short to long-term goals)
6. **Adaptable** (they can adapt easily to different situations and personality types)
7. **Resilient** (they recover from setbacks quickly, learn from situations and do not take rejection personally)

The above traits are what set the top sales performers apart from the journeymen salespeople and as you may have observed, the two sales traits that coincide with the most common entrepreneurial traits mentioned previously, are being **driven** and being **resilient**.

With these two traits as a starting point, it is my true belief that there is a more-than-capable and competent salesperson in every business owner and that every aspiring business owner (even without a sales background) has the potential to be entrepreneurial enough to start their own business and make a success of it.

Having a marketing background or being in a customer facing role will also potentially lend itself well to anyone becoming a competent entrepreneurial seller.

My definitive take on the term entrepreneurial sales is therefore '*a business owner or salesperson taking on a more entrepreneurial approach to sales, in the hope of greater profit*'.

In summary, the formula for becoming an entrepreneurial seller would be:

| Entrepreneurial Mindset | Sales Enlightenment | Entrepreneurial Seller |

Being more sales-enlightened will take you beyond entrepreneurship and allow you to rise above all those other ambitious entrepreneurial small business owners out there who lack any real sales know-how and experience!

Are you sales-enabled and optimised?

Seasoned or 'accomplished' entrepreneurial sellers (see entrepreneurial sales spectrum below) understand which tools and resources they need to fully enable their sales, i.e. Sales Enablement.

They also regularly evaluate their sales performance and selling skills, so that they are consistently at the top of their sales game, i.e. SPO (Sales Performance Optimisation). CSO Insights (the research division of Miller Heiman Group) produces an annual study on the latest SPO trends from an international sample of businesses.

The business owners that I have met and that I consider to be true entrepreneurial sellers by and large possess all these attributes but also display seven other combined behaviours or habits (which are showcased in Chapter 4.

Finally, a big part of succeeding as an entrepreneurial seller is having the right mental approach or 'mindset'. You may be familiar with the saying 'mind over matter', but the mind really does matter when it comes to entrepreneurial sales!

Changing your mindset

Whether you are a small business owner or salesperson aspiring to be a small business owner, a change of mindset is often needed in order to pave the way to becoming a fully-fledged entrepreneurial seller.

The Business Owner: In my dealings with thousands of small business owners over my extensive time in sales, I've found that very few considered themselves to actually be in 'sales'. They had been entrepreneurial enough to start a new business but not too many professed to being sales-focused or sales-engaged!

Given that sales is the lifeblood of any company, it is critical that all small business owner see themselves as being very much 'in sales'. With this change in mindset, sales will become more instinctive and more importantly, more consistent.

The Salesperson: Most salespeople that I've worked with or managed in the past didn't usually consider themselves to be the finished article.

Their sales ability would most certainly have been enhanced if they had opened their mind and taken on a more entrepreneurial approach to how they sold, i.e. been more creative, taken more measured risks and been responsible for developing their own sales acumen (rather than having relied on their employer for development).

Anyone who owns a small business or is in a sales or a customer-facing role can better equip themselves for selling to today's more sophisticated and educated buyer – but this does entail having a thought-through growth strategy, using a sales process and applying some proven selling techniques.

The aim of this book

The ultimate aim of this book is to help small business owners and aspiring small business owners (such as seasoned sales professionals) understand the following:

- Why it's essential to be both entrepreneurial **and** sales-savvy in business
- What the top seven entrepreneurial seller habits or behaviours are
- How you can develop and progress up the entrepreneurial sales spectrum
- How entrepreneurial sales can help you grow your business faster

 TOP TIP: Read through this book thoroughly and make a list of the strategies and techniques that appeal most to your way of working. Persevere with these for at least 3 to 4 months before trying some of the other measures featured in this book.

2. THE ENTREPRENEURIAL SALES SPECTRUM

Before you can determine your entrepreneurial sales potential, you need some form of benchmark: in other words, a reference point to start from.

To this end, I have created a simple entrepreneurial sales spectrum that charts the progressive phases of entrepreneurial sales development.

The points along this scale are based on my observations of working with hundreds of successful entrepreneurs and accomplished sales professionals and this can be used to determine where you are now with your entrepreneurial sales development.

Your position on the spectrum will depend on your previous sales training, your sales experience, your entrepreneurial spirit and your approach to business, i.e. your capacity to spot a good commercial opportunity and then maximise that opportunity.

There are four main points along this spectrum, and these are:

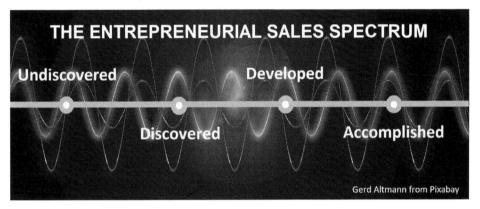

NB. Read the definitions below to gauge where your current position is on the entrepreneurial sales spectrum. Re-assess and revisit your position in six months' time, after you have read this book and implemented some entrepreneurial sales best practice!

The 'Undiscovered Entrepreneurial Seller'

I use this term to describe either a business owner who is inexperienced in sales or a salesperson who is lacking business acumen and some entrepreneurial awareness but potentially looking to start their first business venture (like myself back in 2014).

> *"Mistakes are the usual bridge between inexperience and wisdom."*
> *(Phyllis Grissim-Theroux)*

The Business Owner: The 'undiscovered' business owner is one who is in the very early stages of ownership but perhaps has yet to 'nail down' their product or service offering and hasn't experienced those inevitable speed bumps, hurdles and challenges which all business owners ultimately experience in the first eighteen to twenty-four months of trading.

They are potentially unsure as to how best to pitch their wares or they just haven't given too much thought to being more innovative and diverse, as inevitably most businesses need to do when operating in any evolving or changing market. In other words, their inner entrepreneurial seller lies dormant and is yet to be discovered, developed and liberated.

The Salesperson: The 'undiscovered' salesperson would typically be in their first sales role and still finding their selling feet or may have just switched roles from an account manager type of position. They may have received some rudimentary sales training during their induction and probationary periods, but they haven't worked out yet how they can rise above their fellow sales peers and competitors. Again, their inner entrepreneurial seller lies dormant and is yet to be discovered, developed or liberated.

The 'Discovered Entrepreneurial Seller'

I use this term to describe a business owner or salesperson who has the green shoots of entrepreneurial sales awareness and aspires to be more aware and developed in their present situation or role.

"The real voyage of discovery consists not in seeking new landscapes, but in having new eyes." (Marcel Proust)

The Business Owner: The 'discovered' business owner may be one who is beyond the first two years of trading but perhaps is still refining their product or service offering and has successfully circumnavigated some of those inevitable speed bumps and crossroads that all businesses experience in early years of trading.

They have discovered (in part) how best to pitch their wares and given some thought and application to future innovation or diversification, as most businesses need to do within any shifting market. In other words, their inner entrepreneurial seller is in the early stages of discovery and development and as of yet, unliberated.

The Salesperson: The 'discovered' salesperson would be firmly established in their first or second sales role and have an ambition to take on a more senior sales role. They will have received rudimentary sales training and given some thought to how they can be better than all their counterparts and competitors. In other words, their inner entrepreneurial seller is in the early stages of discovery and development and as of yet, unliberated.

The 'Developed Entrepreneurial Seller'

I use this term to describe a business owner or salesperson who has developed and advanced in their situation, role and expertise.

"Personal development is the belief that you are worth the effort, time and energy needed to develop yourself." (Denis Waitley)

The Business Owner: The 'developed' business owner would be one who is beyond the first five years of trading and has refined their product or service offering, whilst successfully circumnavigating most of those inevitable speed bumps and crossroads that all businesses experience during their early existence.

They've learned how best to pitch their wares and have been able to pivot, when needed, their business by innovating or diversifying, as inevitably most businesses need to do within any shifting market. In other words, their inner entrepreneurial seller is discovered but not fully developed and as of yet, not fully liberated.

The Salesperson: The 'developed' salesperson would be firmly established in a senior or national sales role and have a future ambition to start their own business. They will have received role-specific sales training and sought their own 'self-learning' outside work. They know how they are better than all their counterparts and competitors. In other words, their inner entrepreneurial seller is discovered and developing but as of yet, not fully liberated.

The 'Accomplished Entrepreneurial Seller'

I use this term to describe a business owner or salesperson who has fully developed and now reached the pinnacle of their profession, trade or role.

> *"To be yourself in a world that is constantly trying to make you something else is the greatest accomplishment."* (Ralph Waldo Emerson)

The Business Owner: The 'accomplished' business owner would be one who is beyond ten years of trading and has refined their product or service offering several times over, and has successfully circumnavigated virtually all of those inevitable speed bumps and challenges that all businesses experience. They will also be able to exhibit great skill and flair, within their specific discipline.

They've learned how best to pitch their wares and have been able to pivot their business on a number of occasions through constant innovation or diversification. In other words, their inner entrepreneurial seller is fully discovered, absolutely developed and fully liberated.

The Salesperson: A seasoned salesperson may be at the point of thinking about starting their own business or have already taken the business ownership route with a 'side hustle'. They will have researched or received training outside sales about other business functions, e.g. finance or IT, or taken the decision to outsource these critical functions.

They know how their business concept or fledgling business differs from their competitors. In other words, their inner entrepreneurial seller is discovered, developing and partially liberated but will develop further through the experience of owning their own business. This added dimension of business ownership will help them, in time, to become an accomplished entrepreneurial seller.

Moving up the entrepreneurial sales spectrum

Irrespective of where you feel you are on the entrepreneurial sales spectrum, as a small business owner, being more entrepreneurial and sales-savvy will help you grow personally as a business owner, as well as grow your business.

You can use the strategies, processes and techniques featured in this book to help develop your entrepreneurial mindset and sales skills, with the aim of moving up the entrepreneurial sales spectrum – to the point where you have accomplished what you want for your business and in your work life.

TOP TIP: To become accomplished at something, you have to be consistent in your thinking and your actions. Always plan your actions but be prepared to modify your plans – if the situation dictates. Be consistent in what you do, and this will help embed the behaviours that are needed to be more accomplished.

3. THE 7 DISTINCT HABITS OF ENTREPRENEURIAL SELLERS

In the previous chapter I defined what entrepreneurial sales is and how to gauge where you currently sit on the entrepreneurial sales spectrum. I also touched on the associated habits and behaviours of entrepreneurs and seasoned sales professionals and how these can lead to becoming an entrepreneurial seller.

In this chapter, I am going to define the seven habits that I believe are unmistakeably entrepreneurial seller related. My beliefs are based on having worked with what I believe to be extremely accomplished and successful entrepreneurial sellers, over a relatively long 30 years in both sales and the business world.

These seven distinct entrepreneurial seller habits or behaviours, unsurprisingly, combine some of the traits of an archetypal entrepreneur with the habits that I associate with being a seasoned and successful sales professional.

Entrepreneurial sales criteria

Success, of course, is a relative term and it can mean different things to different people and business owners. The benchmarks I have used are entrepreneurs who have a high level of sales acumen and have launched a number of successful and profitable business ventures.

> *"Success is not the key to happiness. Happiness is the key to success. If you love what you are doing, you will be successful."*
> *(Albert Schweitzer)*

Classic entrepreneurial seller habits are very similar to those associated with an archetypal entrepreneur, e.g. being innovative, passionate, strategic, driven, resilient and a good leader, but with the added dimension of being more sales-focused and customer-centric, i.e. if you look after your customer, then the sales will normally look after themselves!

Any new habit has to be nurtured and then applied consistently for it to stick. If you want to adopt and then engrain any of these entrepreneurial seller habits (or any type of habit for that matter), then here are a few tips for doing that:

- Be clear about your intentions and stick to them
- Create an environment to support your entrepreneurial seller habits
- Get everyone on board with adopting your entrepreneurial sales habit
- Start with mini-steps and then build your entrepreneurial seller habit
- Make your habit standard 'everyday practice' – to make it stick

The seven distinct entrepreneurial seller habits:

1. Passionate Visionary: A entrepreneurial seller will normally have passion in abundance and generally commits themselves fully to whatever they do. An early lesson in sales is that if you don't sell with passion then you can't expect others to get passionate about what you sell? Passion has always been in fashion – when it comes to selling!

Being passionate is contagious and the more passion you show about something, then the more engaging and believable you will be to others (especially when trying to sell them something that is new to them or requires a major investment from them).

The two things an entrepreneurial seller will be most passionate about are their main purpose in life, i.e. what their vision is for their business, and their love of sales. Their vision will be exacting and distinct but also the one thing that helps get them through those inevitable lows of business ownership. Enjoying the 'crack of the deal' (rather than the monetary value) is also something that will stir their blood.

> **"Chase the vision, not the money, the money will end up following you."**
> *(Tony Hsieth – CEO of ZAPOS)*

2. Innovative Strategist: Innovation refers to creating more effective concepts, processes, products and services. It is an integral part of the entrepreneurial seller's DNA and the main catalyst for helping any entrepreneurial seller grow their business and remain competitive.

The world is constantly changing and if, as a small business owner, you don't match that pace of change, then you will eventually become just another failed brand (think Blockbusters).

The UK's lacklustre productivity has been blamed on a number of factors, but one of these factors is the huge numbers of unproductive 'zombie' companies that are not experiencing growth.

A 'State of Small Business Britain' report produced by the Enterprise Research Centre in 2018 showed that only about 36 per cent of SME employers reported turnover growth, meaning that nearly two-thirds (64 per cent) are either just treading water, i.e. stagnating, or actually declining (this last portion estimated at 20 per cent).

This lack of growth is, in my experience, down to a number of different reasons, with low adoption of technology being a major factor but also lack of innovation being another tech-related factor.

Having no clear strategy for adapting to any ever-changing marketplace is another big factor and I've lost count of the number of times I have heard a small business owner proclaim: "I've always done it this way, so I'll carry on doing it this way".

The way to embrace change is to be constantly innovating and the one thing that small agile businesses can do better than their larger (less-agile) rivals is to be able to change tack more quickly and often (if needed). Small businesses can be both proactive and reactive with their evolving strategies.

Having a strategy, i.e. 'a plan of action designed to achieve a long-term or overall aim', is also an essential for testing and implementing each of your innovative ideas.

Any innovation has to fit with your bigger picture, i.e. what is your business strategy and how do you plan to realise that strategy? Whenever formulating a new strategy, just remember to consider the following:

- What is the specific strategy, activity or goal?
- What part does it play in your vision, mission and purpose?
- What is your plan for accomplishing your strategy, activity or goal?
- What type of audience will your strategy, activity or goal reach?
- What results do you expect by implementing your strategy, activity or goal?

> *"Innovation is seeing what everybody has seen and thinking what nobody has thought."* (Albert Szent-Gyorgyi)

Innovative thinking has to be part and parcel of your daily business operation, but it also has to align with your greater business purpose.

3. Measured Risk-taker: Just starting a business means you are taking a risk, so by their very nature, all business owners are risk takers. Entrepreneurial sellers are measured risk takers in that they weigh up the pros and cons of something and gauge how much it will support or contribute towards sales, before deciding to go ahead.

Risks come in different shapes and sizes and some can be complex, whilst others can be more simplistic in their nature. A risk can also be 'unknown' or 'known', whereby the circumstances and ramifications are either not understood or fully understood, i.e. a known risk.

If the end results, outcomes and gains outweigh the initial outlay and associated risks of the opportunity and contribute towards generating revenue, then it is normally worth taking a chance.

Certain risks can be mitigated to improve the odds of you getting a preferred outcome with any given situation, but you will need to apply some proven process:

1. Identify the risk (and relationships within the event or situation)
2. Assess the impacts of the risk (critical consequences, e.g. cost or productivity)
3. Rank risk factors (order from 'most' to 'least' critical)
4. Implement risk mitigation plans (action the 'critical' and track the 'least')

The main context of this is all about sales and revenue-generating opportunities but there are other business-related risks which you should consider:

- Liability (bodily injury to others and their property)
- Property (damage to your company property)
- Business interruption (temporary disruption to your operation)
- Cyber Security (hacking by cyber criminals and data breaches)
- Legal (legal action brought by others for loss of earnings, property etc.)

Experience will eventually help you understand when to take a risk and when not to take a risk but in the meantime, try to avoid risky decisions when you are feeling emotional (as this can cloud your judgement). Postpone any risky decision until your head is clear and you can use reasoned 'emotion free' logic, i.e. embrace your inner Vulcan!

Try not to make a risky decision on impulse either; rather, allow yourself to weigh up the pros and cons first, so you don't regret your decision further down the line and get something akin to 'Buyer's Remorse'.

> *"The biggest risk is not taking any risk ... In a world that is changing really quickly, the only strategy that is guaranteed to fail is not taking risks."*
> *(Mark Zuckerberg – Facebook Founder)*

4. Effective Communicator: Many sellers solve a particular problem for their buyer with the product or service that they sell, and effective problem-solving hinges on understanding and resolving the buyer's problem at hand. You can only really understand the root of the problem and its impact if you are an effective communicator.

2:1 RATIO

Running a viable small business also means communicating and interacting with other stakeholders such as suppliers, investors and other third parties, so an entrepreneurial seller therefore has to also be a good all-round communicator.

Given that over 90 per cent of our communication is through non-verbal cues (body language), it is important to be aware of how we come across to others. Mirroring (mimicking body language), using a firm handshake and sustaining eye contact are all proven techniques for communicating with someone and showing them that you are genuinely engaged.

Using the **2:1 ratio** (you have two ears and one mouth, so use them in that ratio) is also essential – as one of the most important communication skills is actively listening (rather than just passively listening).

Other considerations for effective communication are:

- Be concise and clear about what you are communicating, e.g. use an introductory elevator pitch or write down what you need to communicate and summarise this
- Be observant, i.e. be aware of what the other person is saying (or not saying) and follow the cues from their body language
- Be mindful of the other party's preferred channels of communication, e.g. face to face, conference call, telephone
- Be comfortable with silence: this gives the other party time to process your questions and answers sufficiently and also gives you time to construct your next question.

> **"When the trust account is high, communication is easy, instant, and effective."** *(Stephen R. Covey)*

Communication is an art which needs to be practised – so refine your technique and aim to understand others better, as this will help you communicate more effectively.

5. Persuasive Negotiator: Negotiation is an everyday part of small business ownership – as is persuading others. Persuasion is convincing others to take action and negotiation is discussing a mutually satisfactory agreement, whilst influencing is both persuading and negotiating with others.

Successful negotiation involves the two parties contributing towards the agreed outcome and both parties have to be aware of the other's needs, challenges and demands, i.e. creating a win-win situation for all.

If one party feels that they are disadvantaged or have not equally contributed, then they are more likely to back out of the negotiation there and then or perhaps later on, when they have reflected back on the process, i.e. experienced 'Buyer's Remorse'.

Persuasion can come in a number of guises, e.g.:

Attrition – wearing down the other party into submission, but this can result in the other party getting buyer's remorse because they are not fully committed

Coercion – manipulating someone to do something that they are not entirely comfortable with, which can again lead to buyer's remorse

Education – giving the other the facts and a sound business case for accepting your terms, which allows them to arrive at an informed decision themselves

The last of these, Education, is the most secure and sustainable mode of persuasion. Persuasive negotiators also normally exhibit high levels of self-esteem and emotional intelligence, i.e. the ability to identify and manage their own emotions, as well as tune into the emotions of others.

Other associated effective negotiating attributes include being sincere, authentic, honest, trustworthy, reliable, knowledgeable on your subject matter and offering solutions where there is an opposing view.

> **"Successful negotiation is not about getting to 'yes'; it's about mastering 'no' and understanding what the path to an agreement is."**
> *(Christopher Voss)*

6. Resilient Pragmatist: The definition for resilience is 'the capacity to recover quickly from difficulties; toughness', whilst the definition for pragmatism is 'dealing with things sensibly and realistically in a way that is based on practical rather than theoretical considerations'.

Business owners need a thick 'resilient' skin, just to maintain their business operation, but it is also essential for sales because you will ultimately encounter challenges, get setbacks and experience rejection in both of these aspects of business ownership.

You must be realistic and accepting, i.e. pragmatic, about any setbacks that you get and those inevitable 'No's' that you will experience, otherwise you won't be able to pick yourself up quickly and move forward.

Resilience or pragmatism on their own can be found in many an entrepreneurial business owner or indeed in a sales professional, but the combination of both of these attributes is what, in my opinion, defines an archetypal entrepreneurial seller.

Firstly, there are a number of ways to build business resilience; these include:

1. Not getting distracted from your goal
2. Being clear and decisive in your actions
3. Having a positive perception about yourself
4. Not assuming that all challenges are insurmountable
5. Looking for opportunities where there is change
6. Keeping a balanced perspective, i.e. countering enthusiasm with caution

A simple formula for building resilience in your business is as follows:

1. Identify Risks	2. Mitigate / Avoid Risks	3. Plan Contingencies

Try to identify the risks where you can, avoid them or least mitigate them as much as possible and then have a contingency plan for dealing with any fallout that results.

Being pragmatic comes with practice and experience and a pragmatist will normally see the practical 'upside' in almost any given situation.

There are a number of approaches to being more pragmatic about your business dealings, and these can include:

1. Keeping your dreams realistic, i.e. temper your aspirations with realism
2. Dreaming less by doing more, i.e. actions speak louder than words
3. Looking for practical solutions, i.e. break problems down into smaller more workable components and build a set of mini solutions
4. Adopting continuous improvement, e.g. look to improve your internal processes, your relationships, your business and yourself – continuously
5. Majoring on your strengths, i.e. accept that you will be weaker in some areas than others (check out the 'Strengths Finder' book and website)
6. Seeking out other pragmatists, i.e. learn from others that use pragmatism to make their business better

Building resilience takes time, but as long as you are pragmatic about this and accept that certain things won't happen immediately and that other things will be out of your control, then you can 'compartmentalise' what you can't affect and get on with changing or dealing with what you can affect.

> *"Life doesn't get easier or more forgiving, we get stronger and more resilient."*
> *(Steve Maraboli)*

7. Customer-Centric Seller: Customer-centric selling is very much at the centre of what entrepreneurial sales represents but it requires good communication skills and at times some leadership qualities, e.g. leading indecisive or risk-averse customers along their buying journey or leading a sales team or less experienced sales team member.

Customer-centric selling is all about being there when the buyer is ready to buy and then creating a superior customer experience for that buyer. If, as a seller, you go missing in action, just as the buyer is ready to buy, then they will typically go and buy elsewhere. Buyers want to buy when they want to buy!

They also won't return or recommend you to anyone else if the customer experience they get first time around is disappointing. Even mediocre customer service doesn't 'cut the mustard' for today's more sophisticated and educated buyer.

Good customer service and giving your buyer a good customer experience (CX) has two distinct elements to it:

- **Customer support** (being reactive)
- **Customer success** (being proactive)

Customer support is reacting to inbound customer communications and queries, whereas customer success is being far more proactive by contacting your customer before they contact you, e.g. asking them to give customer feedback via a customer satisfaction survey or scheduling a periodic account review (which also gives you an opportunity to upsell or cross-sell).

> *"If you are not taking care of your customer, your competitor will."*
> *(Bob Hooey)*

There are some considerations to bear in mind with customer-centric selling and these are:

1. **Converse situationally** – instead of using generic presentations
2. **Ask relevant questions** – instead of offering presumed opinions
3. **Focus on the solution** – more than the relationship at first
4. **Target decision makers** – instead of end users
5. **Promote product usage** – instead of focusing on the product alone
6. **Strive to be the best seller** – rather than the busiest seller
7. **Close on the buyer's timeline** – rather than your preferred timeline
8. **Empower buyers to buy** – rather than trying to convince them

Relationship selling is similar to customer-centric selling but there are a number of distinct differences between these two valid sales methodologies.

Customer-centric selling seeks to transform sellers from product pushers to collaborative consultants, whereas relationship selling focuses on the interaction between the buyer and the seller, rather than the price, features and benefits of the seller's product or service.

If your product is very transactional or your customer's buying cycle is short, then it is far more important that you give them a great customer experience, rather than try to build a relationship that takes time, i.e. time the buyer hasn't got.

Conversely, if your sales cycle is much longer and you have the time to build a relationship, then relationship selling will be much more appropriate, but either way, you want the buyer to 'feel' like they have had a great journey and experience.

> *"I've learned that people will forget what you said, people will forget what you did, but people will never forget how you made them feel."*
> *(Maya Angelou)*

Design thinking

Design thinking is not a new concept but it has historically been used by larger organisations, which have larger investment budgets and greater resources.

The concept of design thinking is also more than just hiring a web-developer to build you a great looking website or app; it's really about designing your systems, processes and products or services with the end-user specifically in mind, i.e. your customer.

Design thinking means (as emphasised above) looking at the world through your customer's eyes and really understanding what their experience is like. Once you have this essential customer insight, you can then design, adapt and modify your entire offering to align with your customer's real (and not perceived) preferences.

Being a small business means you will also be agile enough to introduce the necessary alignment changes faster than perhaps a larger (less agile) competitor, but these changes should also include your business structure, i.e. your staffing and business functions, as these will need to be modified as your business scales.

Consider different types of structure – functional, divisional etc. – and figure out which changes will best support your current and projected rates of growth. Using 'matrix of change analyses' will help you identify how your existing and proposed business system changes will impact your overall system. This is represented in the transition matrix section (research 'matrix of change analyses' for further details).

Clear leadership and competent management will be needed to facilitate the necessary phases of structural change for driving future profitable growth – so surround yourself with good people from day one (if you can afford it)!

Focus on personalisation

In the modern world today, consumers (B2B or B2C) prefer a more personalised experience that caters to their exacting needs.

Mundane tasks like purchasing basic goods and services or dining out now need to be more 'experiential' for many buyers (especially millennial buyers). This means personalising your CX so that they feel more valued and therefore more likely to stay with you, spend more with you and recommend you.

Personalising your CX will also help your business stand out from all those other operators that still provide a generic 'one size fits all' approach to servicing customers.

This more recent shift in consumer behaviour is down to a combination of reasons, and these include:

- A global and national economic downturn (less disposable income for consumers)
- A demographic shift (millennial consumers now match baby-boomer consumers)
- Technology (providing convenience and speeding up purchase and delivery)
- Increased competition (especially from online competitors with lower overheads)

Being aware of what is happening at a local 'micro' level as well as what is happening at a wider 'macro' level will help you adapt, change and pivot your business model where necessary, but don't be afraid to change where the demand is there and you know that you can service that demand, e.g. with a few operational tweaks.

Is your perception true?

Remember that your perception of the service you provide to your customers may be at odds with your customers' perception.

Put yourself in their shoes regularly, walk yourself through their buying journey and get their feedback (good or bad), as this is vital insight that can help you adapt your business model and remain viable.

> *"Change the way you look at things and the things you look at change."*
> *(Wayne W. Dyer)*

As an entrepreneurial seller, all you need to remember with customer-centric selling is to put the customer at the centre of your sales (whilst putting sales at the centre of your business).

Why these behaviours complement each other

All of the above behaviours work in tandem for entrepreneurial sales, but possessing good people skills is very much what being an entrepreneurial seller is about.

Whereas leadership appears as one of the top entrepreneurial behaviours, this does not appear as a standalone top entrepreneurial seller behaviour, because an entrepreneurial seller can be a self-employed freelancer or sole trader.

Being an effective communicator does, however, appear in the list of entrepreneurial seller behaviours, as this doesn't just involve influencing buyers but also involves elements of leadership, e.g. engaging with and leading various investors, staff and other stakeholders along the vision that you have for their business venture.

NB. I will be covering these seven distinct entrepreneurial seller behaviours in further detail later (see Chapter 9: 'Developing Your Entrepreneurial Sales Skills').

TOP TIP: **Work on your people skills by really trying to understand others. Listen 'actively' and acknowledge others' positive attributes and expertise. Practise being empathetic and remember to control your emotions in all situations. If you lose your cool, then you have normally lost the argument (and potentially the deal)!**

4. ENTREPRENEURIAL SELLER CASE STUDIES

Since starting my sales consultancy business in 2014, I have been fortunate enough to work with some very successful people in the business world and a number of these I would consider to be true entrepreneurial sellers.

In my personal dealings with all five of the entrepreneurial sellers showcased in this section, I am especially struck by their clear vision, their determination and their drive and of course, their high levels of sales acumen.

I asked these entrepreneurial sellers the same ten sales and business-related questions, so that you can hopefully identify some commonality between their various origins, modi operandi and sales strategies.

PS. I have also added my observations at the end of these profiles!

Emma Jones MBE (Founder of Enterprise Nation & Author)

Emma had a big impact on me when first starting my consultancy business and she continues to do so. At the time, Emma's company (Enterprise Nation) had been awarded the contract to manage a database of advisers for a new government grant scheme called Growth Vouchers. I signed up as an adviser to this scheme by joining Enterprise Nation as one of their accredited members. I have since gone on to work with Emma and Enterprise Nation in a number of additional roles and functions.

Bio: Emma is the founder of Enterprise Nation, a business expert, media commentator and author of bestselling business books such as *Working 5 to 9* and *Go Global*. Emma founded Enterprise Nation in 2005; it supports a growing community of over 70,000 small business entrepreneurs. Prior to this, Emma had her own technology company, which she sold to start up Enterprise Nation.

Q1. Why did you start Enterprise Nation?
"I started Enterprise Nation after selling my first business. The experience of starting, growing, and then selling a business gave me the idea to build a platform and business to support other people to do the same!"

Q2. Who did you start this with, or did you go solo?
"My first business, Techlocate.com, was started with a partner but in Enterprise Nation I'm a sole founder which has its plus points and downsides. It makes for a lonelier growth journey and means it's even more important to surround yourself with really talented people and advisers."

Q3. What was your long-term vision for Enterprise Nation?
"To build what's described in the name! It's been incredible to be part of the flourishing enterprise scene in the UK with record numbers of people starting a business each year. We see our job at Enterprise Nation as supporting people to start and grow a business and our vision is to ensure all small businesses get access to quality support. Building an Enterprise Nation is good for the economy, but also for society as small businesses are shown to make a significant contribution to their local communities."

Q4. How did you raise finance at the start?

"I financed Enterprise Nation through the sale of my previous business. My first business, you'll be pleased to know, was funded by making sales! I'm a big believer in making sales as opposed to raising funds. We waited seven years to raise funds for Enterprise Nation and this was a decision taken as I was ready to scale the business."

Q5. Did you have any sales experience prior to starting this venture?

"I started life waiting tables in my mum's restaurants, which I feel gives the best sales training. You have to ensure your customers are having a great time – and that will flow through to sales! My first and only proper job was with Arthur Andersen, where I joined as a tax accountant but soon moved into business development. You could say I've been selling ever since!"

Q6. Did you have an initial sales plan/target, and did you hit your first target?

"Yes, I still obsess about sales plans and targets. You have to – without it, you simply don't have a business to run. Most years we have hit target. My team can get mad as each year I raise the targets!"

Q7. When did you employ your first sales or customer-facing employee?

"Great question! Enterprise Nation has always hired customer-facing employees, but our first hire dedicated to partnerships and sales was in 2014."

Q8. How do you maintain creativity and innovation in your business?

"The product we are selling is constantly innovating as, for small business, we sell a subscription product that has events and online platform at its heart. Both are continually being refreshed and updated. In terms of our actual sales process, we use CRM and keep weekly track of our pipeline. This doesn't sound very innovative, but I do feel sales success also requires ongoing project management in nudging deals along."

Q9. What do you do outside work – to maintain a good life balance?

"Pretty much the only thing I do 'outside work' is go to the gym and spend time with the family. But I'm terrible at this question as, for me, work/the business/what we're trying to achieve is my life, so I don't begrudge spending a lot of time working on it. You have to do what you love and, for me, it's building a business that hopefully makes a difference to small businesses."

Q10. What advice would you offer a young aspiring entrepreneurial seller?

"Find a mentor! Learn from people who sell well and never stop learning. Also learn to pick yourself up fast from rejection!"

Robin Sieger (Motivational Speaker, Performance Coach & Author)

I was fortunate enough to see Robin speak at an IOD (Institute of Directors) event in London after he re-issued his best-selling book Natural Born Winners in 2014. Robin signed copies of his book at the event and signed my inside cover: 'To Paul, Dream big, dare to fail and create magic. All the best Robin'. His book and friendly words of advice were very inspirational for me and after staying in touch with Robin via LinkedIn, it was great to catch up again recently and interview him for this book.

Bio: Robin Sieger a renowned motivational speaker, an international best-selling author of six books (including Natural Born Winners, which has sold in over 100 countries), a PGA Pro Performance Coach and founder of Sieger International Ltd. In addition, Robin helps schoolchildren develop their self-worth through his 100% NBW International Schools Programme.

Q1. Why did you start Sieger International Ltd?
"I started my business in 1997 with an endgame in mind to build a business that had value beyond me. If your business doesn't deliver value, then it's of no value to anyone."

Q2. Who did you start this with, or did you go solo?
"I went solo because I am a great believer in DIY (Do It Yourself). Because I was on my own, there was no one to fall out with (as can happen in a business partnership) but you can always form strategic relationships – to extend your network and your reach!"

Q3. What was your long-term vision for Sieger International Ltd?
"Creating a 'Go to Business' for training and developing your most important asset – your staff or yourself (if you are self-employed)."

Q4. How did you raise money at the start?
"I started my business in 1997 with a trestle table in the bedroom, my home phone and my savings, so didn't need to raise any initial finance. I then sent out 1,200 personally written prospect letters requesting an interview meeting and that is how I got my first paying client."

Q5. Did you have any sales experience prior to starting?
"Yes, I got a sales job at Manpower (recruitment services) selling 'temp' positions and I also had some Xerox copier training – both of which stood me in good stead for developing my selling skills and knowledge."

Q6. Did you have an initial sales plan/target, and did you hit your first target?
"Yes, it was £40k and this was just to break even. It was a challenging target for a start-up (back then in the 'nineties') but I've always been up for a challenge – as you can see in my best seller 'Natural Born Winners'."

Q7. When did you employ your first salesperson?
"I employed my first salesperson eighteen months after starting my business and he stayed with me for three years, before moving onto a career in the police. Both of these roles involve interacting with and influencing people, so I could see why it was a natural move for him."

Q8. How do you maintain creativity and innovation in your business?
"I'm passionate about helping individuals break through their limiting beliefs and giving them the tools and support to make the step-changes they need in their lives. I apply the same mantra to my organisation – by making sure that we have the right people, tools and resources internally to make the necessary changes for keeping the business fresh and viable."

Q9. What do you do outside work – to maintain a life balance?
"From my time as a stand-up comic (where I was always looking for new material and new challenges), I apply the same outlook to my personal and professional life. I've climbed Ben Nevis before but whatever I do, I commit myself fully and stay the course, otherwise what is the purpose of starting that journey and not finishing it! PS. Always have a destination in mind for any journey!"

Q10. What advice would you offer a young aspiring entrepreneurial seller?
"Commit to your goal or dream, come what may. Don't chase the money but chase the goal – as the money will usually follow!"

Janice B Gordon (Founder of Scale Your Sales & Public Speaker)

I met Janice a few years back at The Business Show, where I caught one of her presentations. I was struck at the time by how polished and engaging her talk was and we spoke afterwards. We have since met up at a number of sales events and Janice recently invited me to guest on one of her sales podcasts. She was an obvious candidate for my entrepreneurial seller case studies, which she kindly agreed to.

Bio: Janice B Gordon is the founder of Scale Your Sales and delivers consultancy and customised client Key Account Management programmes for blue-chip, and mid-cap organisations. Janice is also a published author, renowned public speaker and Visiting Fellow at Cranfield School of Management Centre for Strategic Marketing and Sales.

Q1. Why did you start Scale Your Sales?
"I have always been self-employed on contract or interim. Scale Your Sales has evolved over eight years and the framework rebranded to Scale Your Sales in 2018. If you see a gap in the market you must research then evaluate your niche and the value of the niche. Scale Your Sales helps sales professionals adapt to their specific buyers' preferences and market demands and to futureproof the relationship and revenue."

Q2. Who did you start this with, or did you go solo?
"After being responsible for employees with a partner, I wanted to gain agility and go solo. I work with other independent associates; it allows me to work with a variety of customers and suppliers and tailor the solution to the needs of the customer."

Q3. What was your vision for Scale Your Sales?
"The Scale Your Sales framework will be published in 2020, the podcast launched in 2019. I will continue to grow the consultancy and education platform; the aim is to increase the engagement tenure so the impact of the change can be embedded in not only the sales operation but in the entire organisation. I want the buyers buying from suppliers that they feel they have an affinity and partnership with. I want suppliers aligned to their specific buyers' and customers' wants and needs. I do not see why every company cannot be an Apple in their niche. My aim is to make it happen!"

Q4. How did you raise money at the start?
"I did not need to raise finance in this business unlike others. It is a combination of sweat, personality, experience and intellectual thought."

Q5. Did you have any sales experience prior to starting?
"Yes, I sold my designs when I was 15. I went to America in the 1980s to show my design to get a job and realised I could sell the samples, so I did and made a business out of it. I became an IFA, which is when I got my formal sales training: in the 1990s you could still cold call. After my Cranfield MBA I added breadth to my sales experience with operations, customer experience and digital marketing."

Q6. Did you have an initial sales plan/target, and did you hit your first target?
"Yes, always! It is not possible to manage the strategy of the business without clearly understanding your customer needs and the value you offer your customer and what it is worth to them. Your marketing strategy is making these customers aware of the value and the sales strategy is helping your customer to realise the value. The numbers are easy if you know the values."

Q7. When did you employ your first salesperson?
"I have managed people for many years as a consultant or interim manager. It is very different to when I employed twenty part-time and full-time employees in sales, customer service and operations. When you are responsible for employee motivation and sales management it is difficult to also wear the hat of customer engagement and experience, shareholder and CFO."

Q8. How do you maintain creativity and innovation in your business?
"I take time out of my business in December and January to think, to ask questions, to create the solutions and to plan the strategies of the business."

Q9. What do you do outside work – to maintain a life balance?
"I do yoga, meditation and gym classes, training five to six times a week. I work like crazy ten months of the year and take off December and January to have a working holiday somewhere warm to write or do whatever planned project."

Q10. What advice would you offer a young aspiring entrepreneurial seller?
"Create a sales system and work it daily before you do any other project. Do everything like you could not fail and ask yourself 'have I done everything I could to make it happen?' If the answer is YES, then detach yourself from the outcome."

Brett Akker (Founder of Streetcar and LOVESPACE)

I also met Brett at an IOD event in London and it was early days for his newest business venture, LOVESPACE. I introduced myself and established that Bret was looking to expand his business into the offsite records management space (storing paper records at his secure offsite storage facility). Given that I had a records management background, I was able to provide Brett with some market intelligence on the records management industry. We have stayed in contact since and Brett has very kindly offered me ongoing advice and mentoring for my own business.

Bio: Brett Akker is the co-founder of LOVESPACE and Streetcar, which was sold to US car club competitor Zipcar for £32m in 2010. Brett's other business interests include Winerist (an award-winning travel platform) and Envio (a logistics platform). Brett also advises on the board of several other businesses and provides mentorship to the Centre for Entrepreneurs.

Q1. Why did you start Streetcar or LOVESPACE?
"I read an article in a business magazine about car-sharing schemes in Europe and North America and that what the inspiration for Streetcar. With LOVESPACE, the inspiration came from a discussion with Streetcar's first angel investor. The aim of my new venture was "to do for self-storage what Streetcar did for car rentals" and unlike conventional firms, which rent out a specific storage area, LOVESPACE allows people to store individual items. We also provide delivery to and from our storage sites."

Q2. Who did you start this with, or did you go solo?

"I quit my job at Mars and pooled my savings with my friend from university Andrew Valentine and we co-founded Streetcar in 2004. Even when I was studying economics and law at the University of Durham, I knew I wanted to go into business with Andrew. I co-founded LOVEPACE with Streetcar's first ever angel investor and LOVESPACE started trading in 2012."

Q3. What was your vision for Streetcar/LOVESPACE?

"My vision for both Streetcar and LOVESPACE was to be the 'best in class' for customer service, as I felt that this would differentiate us from the new and existing operators out there. I felt if we could build our brand and service around customer service excellence, then this would stand us in good stead against new entrants or existing operators reacting to us by upping their customer service game."

Q4. How did you raise money at the start?

"The money for LOVESPACE came from myself and Carl August Ameln, my co-founder, as well as Smedvig Capital who had previously invested in Streetcar in 2007. Streetcar was originally funded through savings. Andrew and I put in £70,000 in total, and that was pretty much everything we owned at the time. It lasted around a year and we then raised our first round of external finance."

Q5. Did you have any sales experience prior to starting?

"From university, I started off in recruitment and this was a really good grounding for sales. I then moved onto Mars Confectionery UK, which was well known for the quality of its sales training and spent the next five years there in various sales roles. I finally moved on to become a category manager at a major supermarket for a short time before setting up Streetcar."

Q6. Did you have an initial sales plan/target, and did you hit your first target?

"Yes, I started both companies with a dedicated sales, marketing and finance plan that had a target. The saying goes that 'failing to plan is planning to fail' – so you need to understand want you think you can achieve and a well thought through plan with a realistic target will help you with that. The plan and target for both business evolved and became more accurate over time."

Q7. When did you employ your first salesperson?

"Being from a sales background, the need to employ someone in sales wasn't so urgent for us but we did employ our first B2B salesperson at Streetcar ten months in (after the initial angel investment) and then one year in with LOVESPACE. With both businesses, we also built an exceptionally strong customer service team as, quite often, this is the only human contact our customers have - and they proved to be the best sales team we could possibly have had."

Q8. How do you maintain creativity and innovation in your business?

"I believe in giving people responsibility and autonomy, as well as having an open-door policy. By empowering your people to think for themselves, this automatically promotes creativity and innovation in your business. I call it 'collective creativity'. We also have regular team and company-wide meetings to discuss how to take the business forward."

Q9. What do you do outside work – to maintain a life balance?

"At the beginning (being young and single) I didn't get this right and would regularly work seven days a week. This, of course, is not sustainable but now, being married and having a family, I have a much healthier work life balance. We make sure our staff have a similar healthy balance in their lives too, as overworked, stressed out staff will not be as healthy, happy or productive. I also walk the dogs, go for a run or take in a game at my local football club Brighton & Hove Albion FC - and would encourage everyone to have a healthy leisure-based distraction outside of work. It's vital in order to maintain productivity when you're working."

Q10. What advice would you offer a young aspiring entrepreneurial seller?

"Be fully committed to your business because playing at it (doing it as a side project) will very rarely lead to success. You need to be passionate about what you do as well - because you will have those inevitable ups and downs and your passion will get you through those times. Finally, recognise the importance of sales and don't stop at the marketing. Get a sales system in place (use a sales manual or playbook) and remember to train and develop your people because that's how they will grow. Set realistic sales targets (and adapt them if necessary) because there is nothing more demoralising than missing a target because it is unachievable. Get a good work life balance - as this will sustain your energy and sanity levels."

Liv Conlon (Founder of ThePropertyStagers)

I became aware of Liv through my Enterprise Nation membership. As one of the adviser members at Enterprise Nation, I support and attend a number of their regional events and Liv was booked in to speak at their 'Next Gen Fest London' (inspirational festival for young entrepreneurs). I got in contact with Liv's Mum (Ali) who is a director of the business and Liv kindly agreed to be profiled in this book.

Bio: Liv Conlon was just 13 when she started her first business – selling nail foils imported from China and seven years on, she is now the owner of an interiors company with a turnover of £1m. Liv was named 'The UK Young Entrepreneur of the Year' in 2019 by the FSB and came to my attention, whilst supporting the Enterprise Nation Next Gen Awards.

Q1. Why did you start ThePropertyStagers?

"When my mother Ali struggled to sell her investment property after three months on the market, I had the idea to give the flat a 'show home' makeover. I knew about 'staging' as a concept and decided to engage a staging service. However we couldn't find anyone who offered this service at an affordable price, so I decided to do it myself. Within three days it had sold above the valuation and we made a nice healthy profit on the furniture to boot…and so ThePropertyStagers was born! We now furnish around 300 properties per year in the UK."

Q2. Who did you start this with, or did you go solo?

"I started the company completely alone at 16 when I left school. I think it can be great to have a business partner though, but it has to be the right one. My mum now works with me and it's so much better, it is a lot less lonely having someone who can relate to you."

Q3. What was your vision for ThePropertyStagers?

"My long-term vision for ThePropertyStagers has always been to change the way the UK property market presents properties. I wanted to operate nationally, which we do, but our brand is now internationally recognised."

Q4. How did you raise money at the start?

"I didn't have any finance when I started TPS and until this day - have never taken any form of loan or investment into the business. We have a bank overdraft which is a great safety net and it has supported us through times of real expansion."

Q5. Did you have any sales experience prior to starting?

"I had absolutely no sales experience apart from my eBay business selling nail foils – which I set up when I was 13."

Q6. Did you have an initial sales plan/target, and did you hit your first target?

"When I first started in business, my biggest aim like most businesses when they start, is to just start trading and see the money coming in. A year into the journey, this is when I became quite obsessed with goal setting and vision boards. At the time, I had aimed to turnover 30K in 2018, we actually turned over £1m. How's that for smashing your target!"

Q7. When did you employ your first salesperson?

"My mum left her business to join me about 18 months into my journey and she was my first team member. We took on our 2nd team member 6 months later."

Q8. How do you maintain creativity and innovation in your business?

"I'm an extremely creative person and always have been. This is where I feel most in my flow and my zone of 'genius'. I keep it alive by taking several days in the week where all I do is create, whether working on marketing, new ideas or branding. I also do a lot of personal development and invest a lot of my time and money into being mentored by those more successful than me. So, I spend a lot of time on calls and constantly being pushed to be better than yesterday."

Q9. What do you do outside of work – to maintain a life balance?

"At the moment, I wish there was more balance. Business still takes up most of my time (as I'm so driven) and I'm currently focusing my goals. I do make time for myself. I go to the gym and spa every day and try to switch off at weekends too."

Q10. What advice would you offer a young aspiring entrepreneurial seller?

"I would say to them to start a business they are passionate about, as when times are tough, you've got to love what you are doing. I would also say, don't let anyone dim your light or judge you for your age, it may not seem like it now but it will work to your advantage very soon!"

Summary

Whilst all of the above business owners are clearly 'accomplished' entrepreneurial sellers and, in my opinion, demonstrate the seven distinct habits associated with entrepreneurial sales (see page 21 for these) – they are from completely different sectors and backgrounds.

As regards to what else they have in common, all of them, I would say, have similar personalities in that they have a measured steely determination but are all also very humble, approachable and what I would call 'People's People'. They are motivated and can also motivate others, which is essential for growing or scaling a business.

They have all been more than happy to offer their 'worldly' advice freely for this book and clearly have a natural motivation for helping others. This is demonstrated by their philanthropic, coaching and mentoring commitments, which all of them have outside of their main business interests.

They have either held a former sales position before staring their business venture, run a side hustle or at least received some formal sales training or mentoring. It is also clearly important for all of them that they continue to grow by developing their own sales knowledge, know-how and acumen.

All of them started their businesses by bootstrapping (using savings, bank overdrafts, credit cards etc.) and then later seeking financial investment. Clearly, none of them wanted to overreach themselves financially – in those crucial early months.

Robin, Emma and Janice have written at least one best-selling book each, whilst Brett and Liv have contributed to a number of collaborative publications. I asked Brett and Liv if they had 'a book inside them' and whilst both said they did – they just do not have the time right now to sit down and write one.

All of them, as you would expect, are passionate about sales, truly love their work and are dedicated to their business but enjoy their downtime, when they can get it!

TOP TIP: **Make sure to always communicate your passion. This is what will get others to 'buy' into what you do and what you sell. Aim to be not just the best version of yourself but also the best expert or authority in your particular field. This is what will earn you brand awareness, positioning, respect, trust and more customers.**

5. THE FEARFUL SMALL BUSINESS OWNER

Not all entrepreneurs are sales-savvy and not all experienced salespeople have the ambition to become an entrepreneurial business owner. This is because we all have different aspirations.

My aspiration is to have a reasonably comfortable lifestyle, a good work-life balance but not create a business empire, which can mean a lot of personal sacrifice. For others, it is the exact opposite i.e. they want to be the next big IT industrialist or media mogul.

In my experience, a lack of skills or acumen is not the thing that stops someone taking the first steps to realising their ambitions and becoming a more sales-savvy and entrepreneurial business owner, i.e. an entrepreneurial seller – it's actually a combination of natural born fears!

> *"Nothing in life is to be feared, it is only to be understood. Now is the time to understand more so that we may fear less."*
> *(Marie Curie)*

Fear is one of the most primeval emotions known to mankind and one of the biggest things that can hold anyone back from achieving what they want most in life.

As an aspiring business owner, you may have identified a gap in a market, have a brilliant idea that will service that gap and be forward thinking and prepared enough to take a number of measured risks to get your business venture off the ground, i.e. the archetypal definition of an entrepreneur, but if you have any nagging doubts about coming up short, then those doubts can be enough to put many people off trying in the first place.

If you haven't got a sales background either (as with the majority of small business owners) and don't know how to market and sell your idea, then this lack of sales know-how can breed fear, which in turn will affect you and your fledgling business venture from getting that crucial early traction.

Fear comes in many guises

The most common 'fear' factors that I see with people who are planning their first business venture or are in the start-up phase of their company are a fear of:

1. Failure
2. Being overwhelmed
3. Running out of money
4. Not being seen (or heard)
5. The unknown
6. Success

1. Fear of failure: Whilst all of the above six fears are closely linked, fear of failure is the most common fear that I see amongst aspiring, start-up or early-stage business owners. Fear of failure can come in many guises, from being worried about failing at one particular aspect of your business, e.g. raising sufficient funds at the beginning or perhaps not generating enough sales to get that vital early traction, to a fear of the complete business failing all together.

Small business owners will experience 'micro-failures' on an almost daily basis and these micro-failures can range from wasting part of a marketing budget on an ill-conceived advertising campaign to an important sale falling through at the last minute or even an array of deadline related issues such as missing a planned launch for a new seasonal product or service.

The trick is to accept that these micro-failures will happen and are all part of the learning curve for an entrepreneurial seller. Once you accept that things won't always go right and that many things are outside your control, then these fears will lessen sufficiently for you to push through them.

PUSH

THROUGH

YOUR

FEARS

Image by Pedro Figueras from Pixabay

Failure is only final if you let it become so; otherwise, it's just a temporary pause in your business journey. Acceptance and learning to let go will help you deal with all those inevitable micro-failures that affect all types of business owner, whether novice or seasoned!

> *"When we give ourselves permission to fail, we, at the same time, give ourselves permission to excel."*
> *(Eloise Ristad)*

2. Fear of being overwhelmed: This particular fear will apply more to some than others, depending on your personality type and levels of resilience. Entrepreneurship isn't easy and becoming an entrepreneurial seller (with the added focus of generating more consistent sales) is even harder to start with.

Obstacles will present themselves on a regular basis and having the patience, resilience and skillset to deal with these is a natural progression. Stress levels can also play a part in this progression process.

The trick to dealing with feelings of 'overwhelm' is to remember that you are in control of yourself and master of your own destiny. Many people choose business ownership because of the freedom it brings and the fact that they are answerable only to themselves – so, ultimately, you only have to answer to yourself.

If you need to outsource some of your work, then it has never been as easy to do so. If the person you've outsourced to isn't producing, then you can fire them and find someone else who is up to the task.

Sharing your feelings with a business mentor or trusted business associate will also often shed new light on an issue that you thought was previously insurmountable.

There are many ways to deal with feeling overwhelmed, so you just have to find the right formula and coping mechanisms that work best for you.

> *"Trials and tribulations of every kind are what give us the strength to rise above and find success."*
> *(Lisa Lieberman-Wang)*

3. Fear of running out of money: Finance and funding is another common issue for some and whilst 'fear of not raising enough capital' is high up the fear list, another related fear is running out of working capital.

Many start-up businesses 'bootstrap' at the beginning, i.e. they use savings, max out the credit card, raid their bank overdraft or borrow from friends and family – but eventually these channels of accessible finance can dry up.

If a fear of running out of money is what's preventing you from taking your business forward, then there are far more finance options available to you now, including:

1. **Traditional Bank Loans** – the 'Bank Referral Scheme' also means that banks are legally obliged to help you find funding elsewhere if they turn your loan application down.

2. **Crowdfunding**, i.e. raising funds from the general public via online platforms where people can either lend you money (peer-to-peer lending) or take a stake, i.e. shares or equity, in your business.

3. **Angel Investors or Venture Capitalists** who will both lend you money in exchange for equity (shares), but venture capitalists will normally loan you more.

4. **Short-term Loans** (or payday loans) from finance companies, which can help bridge a short-term financial gap, but interest rates are always high.

5. **Guaranteed Loans** is an alternative route for those that cannot put up security or have an established trading history, but you will need to find a third party to guarantee your loan and take on the loan liability.

6. **Incubator or Accelerator Loans**, e.g. the government-backed StartUp Loans Company, which will provide seeding and mentoring for ambitious start-ups; there are also other government-backed loan options.

7. **Grants**, e.g. research and development money that is either provided in full or in part ('match-funded'); you may have to find half of the money yourself.

> *"Successful people make money. It's not that people who make money become successful, but that successful people attract money. They bring success to what they do."*
> *(Wayne Dyer)*

4. Fear of not being seen (or heard): This is all about branding. If you operate in a competitive sector dominated by major brands or long-established operators, then trying to be seen (or heard) could be your biggest challenge and therefore your biggest fear.

Building a brand won't happen overnight but you can speed up the process by being consistent and having a proper branding strategy. Brand is more than just your company logo – it's what others think about you and their perception of you and your company. Your brand strategy should therefore include:

1. **Knowing who your target market is**, i.e. your ideal customer type/types
2. **Knowing who the other brands are** in your market (your competitors)
3. **Understanding your value proposition** (the reasons why people buy from you) and distilling this into a brand mission or value proposition statement
4. **Building your brand capital** – corporate colours, logo, tagline, elevator pitch, personal style, blogging style, website design and look of marketing materials etc.
5. **Communicating the right brand message** to your target market – using the right marketing channels

Becoming known as an expert in your field or being recognised as a trusted brand does take time but you also have to be consistent in what you do.

This means adhering to the **Know**, **Like**, **Trust** formula, i.e. people need to get to know you first before they like you enough to trust you – then once they trust you, they will do business with you. Try to design your marketing around this formula.

> *"We do not fear the unknown. We fear what we think we know about the unknown."* *(Teal Swan)*

The aim of your business plan should be to address some of the usual challenges that all businesses face. You may not have faced some of these challenges yourself before but your plan will prompt you to think about these, ahead of them happening.

It should also contain a set of strategies for getting you started, but most small businesses will have to adapt and evolve this set of strategies to adapt to a constantly changing market. As mentioned previously, this can mean completely having to pivot your business model (based on the supply and demand within your market).

Belief is the biggest thing that will help you conquer your fear of the unknown. Remind yourself constantly of your higher purpose (your reasons for doing what you do) and as long as you keep faith in your business model and your own abilities, then most unforeseen challenges can be overcome either by yourself or with help from others.

Using a bit of technique can help too, i.e. chunk down any unforeseen challenge into smaller parts and build a plan to tackle these now more manageable parts, and do this in a logical working order.

Also tap into your business circle or mentoring channel, to get some fresh and impartial perspective on the challenge. Talking to fellow business owners that operate in different markets can sometimes offer some alternative 'best practice'.

Finally, visualising success (which is what many elite sportspeople do) can help you maintain the belief that any challenge, obstacle or problem can be overcome.

6. Fear of Success: Many are conditioned from an early age to strive for success and according to the eminent psychologist Erik Erikson, each of our personal stages of development focuses on achieving success in the different aspects of our life.

Image by Free-Photos from Pixabay

Conversely, we encounter people that tell us that we will not be a success. This negative type of mental conditioning (which can come from a dispassionate parent, teacher or sibling – perhaps trying to mean well) can then instil a limiting type of self-belief that is carried through to adulthood. Typically, people with lower self-esteem or lower levels of confidence may well have been subject to this type of negative mental conditioning earlier in their lives.

Being told that you won't be successful can drive some people on to greater success, because they have the drive to want to 'prove the doubters wrong' – but for others, it can have the opposite effect.

Those who think that other important people in their lives have no faith in them often feel that the odds are stacked against their success and that external forces will always impede their development. They may also be at greater risk of fearing the notion of success, too.

It may be that this type of person does not feel their success has been earned (which is often referred to as 'Imposter Syndrome') and the dictionary definition for this is:

'The persistent inability to believe that one's success is deserved or has been legitimately achieved as a result of one's own efforts or skills'

The term Imposter Syndrome was coined by clinical psychologists Pauline Clance and Suzanne Imes in 1978, when they found that despite having evidence of accomplishments, people with the syndrome remained convinced that they didn't deserve the success that they were experiencing.

Often sufferers will put their success down to luck or good timing and dismiss it as others believing they were more competent than they actually were.

Whilst early psychological research focused on high-achieving women, the syndrome was actually found to impact men just as much and in similar numbers.

Getting professional help

A small number of people can fear both success and failure at the same time. This is very debilitating for a business owner, as every choice they make must be weighed against both of these fears.

Business owners in this situation can become paralysed with indecision and unable to make any decision or choice at all.

Both fear of success and failure tend to respond well to professional treatments such as NLP (Neuro-Linguistic Programming), CBT (Cognitive Behavioural Therapy) and EFT (Emotional Freedom Technique).

All of these techniques aim to 'overwrite' these damaging self-beliefs and help the person learn new ways of thinking about their future choices. In order to treat any pattern of negative thinking syndrome or disorder you first have to recognise that you have an issue and that you want to do something about it.

The NHS should be your first port of call for checking if there is an underlying mental health issue, and you can access local clinical help by visiting the NHS UK website: *https://www.nhs.uk/using-the-nhs/nhs-services/mental-health-services/how-to-access-mental-health-services/*

 **TOP TIP:** **Make sure to always communicate your passion. This is what will get others to 'buy' into what you do and what you sell. Aim to be not just the best version of yourself but also the best expert or authority in your particular field. This is what will earn you brand awareness, positioning, respect, trust and more customers.**

6. THE BUSINESS CASE FOR ENTREPRENEURIAL SALES

The business case for a business owner becoming more entrepreneurial and sales-savvy is powerful, because being confident in your ability to maintain a healthy top line addresses one of the major fears that most small business owners have.

The same can also be said for a seasoned salesperson who aspires to have their own business (as I did back in 2014) and who will therefore need to adopt a more entrepreneurial mindset before launching their first business venture.

The business case for the business owner

Your sales experience, the size of your business and the stage that your business is at – e.g. start-up, early-stage, mature, – will determine your level of entrepreneurial sales development.

UK Government data from BEIS (Department for Business, Energy & Industrial Strategy) shows that in 2017, there were 5,687,230 private sector SME businesses, up by 197,000 or 4 per cent since 2016. Whilst this increase suggests a continued increase in entrepreneurial growth, top line growth is another matter.

ONS (Office for National Statistics) data shows that the average UK micro business (0 to 9 employees – accounting for 96 per cent of all SMEs), turned over £331,489 in 2017. This was up on 2016's figure of £312,598 – an increase of £18,891 (6.04 per cent growth).

UK small businesses (10 to 49 employees – accounting for 4 per cent of all SMEs) turned over an average of £2,661,924, which was a decrease of £183,568 on 2015's figure of £2,845,492 (-6.45 per cent). Two very different stories from closely related sizes of business.

The value of a business (irrespective of size) is directly related to turnover and net profit. If you increase your turnover, i.e. sales, then you ultimately increase the value of your business.

This is especially important if a business owner has a strategy to exit and sell their business and therefore wants to maximise their return on their investment.

> *"As much as you might love running your business, you must have an end-goal in the plan. At the very least, an exit strategy keeps you from turning your business into a glorified job."*
> *(Kevin J. Donaldson)*

According to research by online business transfer agent Bizdaq, the average UK small business was worth £90,000 in 2017. This has fallen £4,000 from £94,000 in 2016 but is up on 2015's figure of £89,000.

Factors such as continued austerity, market uncertainty, falling levels of consumer spending and increased business costs are adversely affecting the values of UK small businesses, leaving owners unable to reach the true value of their business.

The stages of business growth

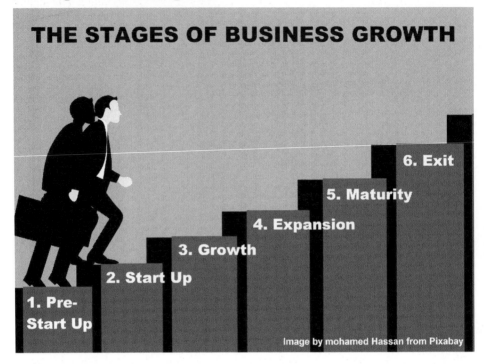

THE STAGES OF BUSINESS GROWTH

6. Exit

5. Maturity

4. Expansion

3. Growth

2. Start Up

1. Pre-Start Up

Image by mohamed Hassan from Pixabay

Every business owner has a vision for their business growing but the size and rate of growth is dependent on many factors.

1. Pre-Start Up: This stage involves the development of your business concept and asking yourself the following questions:

1. Does my concept/idea/product meet a need in the market?
2. Does that market have growth potential, is already growing or saturated?
3. Is my concept/idea/product feasible and profitable?
4. How will I structure and fund my business?

Many concepts and ideas do not pass this four-question test but if the answer is yes, then the next stage is to write a business plan, with a view to starting your business.

2. Start Up: This is probably the most stressful stage of business ownership and many call it a day here. Typical start up challenges include raising investment, finding the right staff, gaining traction with sufficient sales and new customers and 'spinning' all of those other plates that you didn't have to when you were an employee. It is estimated that 20 per cent of start-ups fail in year one and 30 per cent in year two.

3. Growth: This can happen in earnest after the second year but will depend on the type of business. By way of example, vineyard owners in the UK (of which there are now over 500) have to wait three years for their first harvest and then the best part of another year to produce and bottle their wine. Their first harvest is, of course, also dependent on the weather, so this would need to be factored into their plans. Most growth challenges come from managing change, e.g. getting new systems in place, growing head count, growing revenues and maintaining competitiveness.

4. Expansion: This stage is categorised by increasing market share, increasing channels to market, diversifying into new markets, more collaboration and higher adoption of technology. Investment can also be a challenge if the company has an ambitious expansion plan, but merger and acquisition can come into play here. It is estimated that 50 per cent of early stage businesses would have failed by year five.

5. Maturity: This stage is the realisation of the original business concept. Operations and growth are now stable but the biggest challenge with this stage is 'what next'. If growth becomes sluggish, then the business owner will have to drop back down into the mindset of the growth and expansion stages. The business owner should also be thinking about an exit strategy and finding a suitable buyer. If it is a family owned business (of which two-thirds in the UK are), then the founder should be aiming to pass down a viable and profitable business to the next generation. It is estimated that 70 per cent of small businesses would have failed by year ten.

6. Exit: This stage is about executing your exit strategy. Strategies include acquisition, merger, IPO or shutting down operations, i.e. letting the business die. A well-executed exit strategy gives a business owner the means to re-invest in a new business venture or invest in their retirement plans. Always seek professional advice from accredited professionals before deciding what to do with your 'pride and joy'!

As stated earlier, data shows that micro businesses are faring far better than small businesses on the growth front. If small business owners were able to replicate their micro-business-owner counterpart's performance, then this would make a significant difference to the UK national economy.

Is this difference down to micro businesses having greater agility and smaller business costs or are micro-business owners just more entrepreneurially minded and sales-savvy, i.e. entrepreneurial sellers?

Businesses that are generating more sales and profits will be less dependent on having to secure funding. Their cash flow will also be more consistent, and they will be able to attract more talent and pay the necessary wages to retain their talent. In addition, they will be able to invest more in innovation and technology – the drivers that will assist a business in keeping up with their customers' buying preferences and ever-changing market conditions. In other words, look after your sales and your sales will look after your business!

Going niche

A 2017 'SME Strategies for Success' global study produced by Oxford Economics identified the 'Four Aces' of future business success as being:

1. **Applying technology**
2. **Agility**
3. **Accelerating innovation**
4. **Acquiring top talent**

SMEs can use these 'four aces' to position themselves for delivering sustained financial performance and competing successfully against larger or more-established competitors.

The study goes onto conclude that for expanding sales, many SMEs should target specific niche markets where they offer distinct advantages and can avoid having to compete solely on cost, i.e. against larger enterprises with greater economies of scale. "If SMEs can identify a specific niche and deliver high-quality products, they can thrive on small volumes with high margins," says contributor Professor Luca Landoli from the University of Naples.

Being agile enough to target new niche markets is a trait common to most small businesses but entrepreneurial sellers can make the most of these new opportunities with a less risk-averse, but more sales-orientated market approach.

Expansive thinking – not being confined to practices just within your niche – is also the key to developing new opportunities and this is covered in more detail within Chapter 9 'Developing Your Entrepreneurial Sales IQ'.

The business case for the aspirational salesperson

The proportion of UK businesses that employ people has fallen since 2000 from around a third to around a quarter. This decline in the number of employers as a proportion of all businesses is due to the growth in self-employment, with sole proprietors growing by more than the number of all businesses (by 84 per cent, compared with 59 per cent for all businesses).

Monster (recruitment specialists) state that sales related jobs account for 10 per cent to 20 per cent of the UK's total employment and Statista data shows that there are 934,000 employed and self-employed sales, marketing and associated professionals in the UK (this is a slight decrease on the 961,000 high of 2015).

Glassdoor also maintains that 68 per cent of salespeople plan to look for a new job in the next twelve months – so a number of these (especially senior salespeople) will be thinking about pushing out on their own and starting a new business venture. Adding an entrepreneurial string to their sales bow will certainly help a salesperson and wannabe business owner be more innovative when bringing any new business venture to market.

One of the hardest facets for any new start-up business is generating sales – so this will be one less consideration for a seasoned 'out and out' salesperson.

Get a business mentor

Where a salesperson aspiring to be an entrepreneurial business owner can fall down is with all the other business functions that they previously took for granted (because they were looked after by their employer). Administration, Finance, Operations, IT and HR all fall under the remit of a new business owner (especially the self-employed) and the option to delegate, outsource or employ someone (DOES) can be a luxury in the early 'bootstrapping' days of a fledgling start-up business.

This is where a mentor can make a real difference, i.e. someone who has experienced real business ownership pain. Business mentors can be found through local networking or community events, through an introduction from a third party or by drawing up a prospect list of potential 'matches' and then nurturing a relationship with those matches, but remember the adage 'talk but don't stalk' – as not every potential mentor will have the time or inclination to mentor you!

Another mentoring route is to get some support through a professional industry body or business support group.

Industry related institutes and associations such as The Institute of Directors (of which I am a local branch ambassador), can provide many resources to help professional sector businesses, and small business support groups like Enterprise Nation are an ideal 'one stop shop' for SME start-up and early stage businesses. Enterprise Nation now has a community of 70,000 members, supported by a 9,000 strong adviser member network (of which I am one).

Being 'sales ready' is a given with any new small business owner who has a sales background, but salespeople can use the experience and guidance of a trusted business mentor to help them with the challenges of managing all those other 'non-sales' business functions.

Coaches ask questions...

MENTORING

Mentors give answers

Image by Pete Linforth from Pixabay

A business coach can help just as much as a mentor, but whereas mentors advise you, coaches encourage you to come up with the answers yourself.

Business coaches are by their very nature generalists, i.e. they can help you with every aspect of your business, but most come from one particular sector or industry – so this is where their specialist knowledge and know-how will lie.

Before employing any business coach, make sure that they have a good working knowledge of your particular industry, and also check their testimonials.

Finally, there are specialists like me who can help you with one specific aspect or function of your business. As a sales specialist, I predominantly help the majority of small business owners who do not have a sales background – but there is a wealth of expertise out there to help you with your other business functions, such as finance, HR, IT and production.

Conclusion

The business case for being both more entrepreneurial and sales-savvy is an a powerful one. Typically, most business owners want to generate more sales, in order to make more profit and grow their business.

With this in mind, there is clearly a justification for being more entrepreneurially minded and sales-focused, i.e. an entrepreneurial seller. It is also a means to an end for achieving greater wealth and greater success.

 TOP TIP: Being more entrepreneurially minded will help you evolve your business and being more sales-focused will help you generate more consistent and predictable sales. If you are still not convinced about the concept and business case for being more entrepreneurial sales minded, then please read on further.

7. UNLOCKING YOUR ENTREPRENEURIAL SALES POTENTIAL

Being able to unlock your inner entrepreneurial sales potential is all about stimulating the mind to tap into your hidden potential and then using a number of proven tools and techniques to help hone your newly found entrepreneurial sales skills.

> *"If you can change your mind, you can change your life."*
> *(William James)*

We have already spoken about needing to change your mindset and this is essential for accessing any potential that you have within yourself.

Most of us have, at some time, been told by a family member, trusted mentor or caring boss that we have the potential to achieve far greater things in life or at work, and if we were able to channel the necessary focus, dedication and discipline to unlock this potential and apply it, then we would undoubtedly be more successful!

Using your mind's potential fully could benefit you in all areas of your life and at work, from achieving your career goal aspirations to strengthening your personal or working relationships and being far more content and fulfilled with your life.

Putting in the effort needed to unlock your hidden entrepreneurial sales potential is therefore a worthwhile personal investment.

Rebalancing your brain function

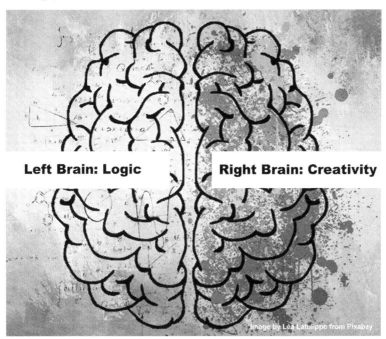

Left Brain: Logic   **Right Brain: Creativity**

Image by Léa Latulippe from Pixabay

There is the theory of 'left brain' and 'right brain' thinking (originating from the work of Roger W. Sperry) which states that each of the two sides (hemispheres) of our brain performs different functions.

The left brain, it is argued, is for language and logic, i.e. performing analytical and objective tasks, whilst the right brain is for creativity, special awareness and visual comprehension, i.e. performing intuitive, thoughtful and subjective tasks.

It can be that a person may have a stronger leaning towards one particular side of the brain, but more recent research has shown that results in subjects such as maths are better when both halves of the brain work together.

Neuroscientists have also established that the two sides of the brain normally collaborate to perform a broad range of tasks and that the two hemispheres communicate through the corpus callosum (a broad band of nerve fibres joining the two hemispheres of the brain).

Left brain thinking

As the left hemisphere of the brain is for logical thought process, this can aid an entrepreneurial seller for:

- **Critical thinking** (gaining early traction with the business)
- **Language** (using the right brand message and marketing speak)
- **Reasoning** (understanding and measuring a risk)
- **Numbers** (managing the top line and bottom line)

This is a crucial element to raising funds, generating sales, managing cash flow and analysing KPIs, i.e. gaining traction and scaling a business.

Right brain thinking

The right side of the brain is for creativity and awareness, so this can aid an entrepreneurial seller with:

- **Recognising faces** (when out networking)
- **Expressing emotions** (when building rapport and relationships)
- **Using intuition** (when taking a measured risk is borderline)
- **Using imagination** (to visualise your company's vision and success)

This is a crucial element for building a brand, building relationships with investors, strategic partners, suppliers and customers and having a grand vision for the final destination of your company.

> *"You have two hemispheres in your brain – a left and a right side.*
> *The left side controls the right side of your body and right controls*
> *the left half. It's a fact. Therefore, left-handers are the only*
> *people in their right minds." (Bill Lee)*

Understanding your strengths and weaknesses

More modern research now suggests that the left brain, right brain theory is in some ways inaccurate, given that both hemispheres work in collaboration on many tasks. It is still, however, important to understand where your strengths and weaknesses lie, so that you can adopt better suited measures for honing your entrepreneurial sales skills.

Many people have a stronger leaning towards a particular style of learning, i.e. visual, auditory or kinaesthetic, so understanding your most preferred learning style can aid your personal development greatly.

An example of this would be a person that perhaps had difficulties in following verbal instructions (often cited as a right-brain characteristic). They would certainly benefit by writing down instructions and concentrating on developing their organisational skills.

The language you use can give a clearer indication as to where your preferred learning style lies. Visual people have been known to say, 'I see what you mean', whilst auditory people may say 'I hear what you're saying' and kinaesthetic people may say 'I know how you feel'.

These observations are not a definite, but paying attention to how you link your sentences and how others do the same can give you a good indication about a preferred learning style.

If you are taking one of the many online left brain/right brain quizzes, then it should be taken with 'a pinch of salt' and don't place too much importance on the results. You are better off taking a VAK learning style quiz (Visual, Auditory, Kinaesthetic) and supplementing this with something like the 'Strengths Finder' assessment (which lists 34 potential strengths and identifies your top five – with suggestions for making better use of these in your life and work).

Rewiring your thought processes

There are numerous self-help books out there that use many different forms and psychology to show you how to unlock any dormant mental potential for achieving greater personal success.

An entrepreneurial seller should be able to harness the power of both sides of their brain – even if they have a perceived natural leaning towards one over the other.

The power of the mind

As an accredited EFT (Emotional Freedom Technique) coach, I know the power of psychology, and when this is coupled with acupressure (as is the case with EFT) it can have a more powerful effect on changing the mind.

> *"Your subconscious mind...knows the answers to your problems and it already knows how to heal you."* (Dr Jill Carnahan)

NLP (Neuro-Linguistic Programming), CBT (Cognitive Behavioural Therapy) and hypnosis are other forms of therapy that can help address long-standing limiting beliefs, disorders and syndromes, but most people typically look to these alternative routes if they are in need of professional counselling.

An eminent psychologist, Dr Chris Gilbert, MD, PhD, has written for Psychology Today about accessing your inner genius and references people with 'savant syndrome'. These people have, at some time, suffered a head injury or had an illness such as a stroke that affected their left anterior temporal lobe (LATL). This is the part of the brain that suppresses our full abilities and potential, to help us focus on our primary needs for survival.

Their head injury then has the effect of inhibiting the LATL and this unlocks new skills and genius that previously lay dormant. Dr Gilbert then goes onto explain that healthy people can achieve the same result as savant syndrome sufferers by engaging in activities such as transcendental meditation, repeating mantras or using self-hypnosis, which allows the brain to hyper focus on small less significant details, which will then loosen the oppressive grip that the LATL has on our brain function.

Repetition and habit are other ways to engrain new thinking which will assist you in accessing and utilising your newly found entrepreneurial sales skills. Use the Pareto 80:20 rule to concentrate 80 per cent of your spare time and resources on the top 20 per cent of activities that are most likely to improve your skillset.

Is positive thinking the answer alone?

Positive thinking is important for setting a vision and mission for your business and also for helping you through tougher times.

Recent research has shown that optimism can extend your lifespan and that optimistic people are more resilient to setbacks and managing stress (compared with negative or more pessimistic people).

Positive thinking alone can fool our minds into thinking that we have already resolved a problem or attained our goal and this in turn can lessen our ability to actually achieve our desired outcome.

Fantasy or expectation?

Gabriele Oettingen, who is the professor of psychology at New York University and the University of Hamburg, has written a number of books on the subject of positive thinking and she identifies what she calls two types of positive thinking: fantasy and expectation positive thinking.

Fantasy positive thinking is all about 'dreaming' about your success, and whilst this can calm your mental state – it is proven to measurably reduce your systolic blood pressure – it can also divert your energies and attentions from actually achieving your desired goal.

Expectation positive thinking is more about holding yourself accountable to your actions and endeavours, i.e. expecting success of yourself through your actual deeds.

Professor Oettingen goes on to offer an alternative to positive thinking which she refers to as 'Mental Contrasting'.

Mental contrasting

Mental contrasting combines elements of positive and negative thinking. This approach combines the expectation part of positive thinking with the realism and pragmatism associated more with negative thinking.

Studies have found that this hybrid mental approach can be more effective than positive or negative thinking alone.

Mental contrasting follows this process:

| 1. Focus on your desired goal | 2. Imagine your goal coming true | 3. Now let your mind wander | 4. Consider the obstacles | 5. Plan how to overcome these |

Professor Oettingen uses the acronym WOOP (Wish, Outcome, Obstacle, Plan) for her mental contrasting process, and this can be a more effective way of managing your expectations whilst dealing with those inevitable challenges.

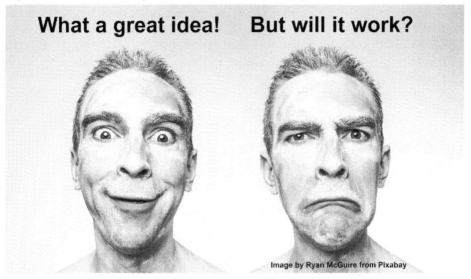

What a great idea!   But will it work?

Image by Ryan McGuire from Pixabay

Ultimately, if you balance any new optimistic idea, concept, aim or ambition with a healthy dose of pessimism, i.e. question what the negatives might be, then you can come to a more balanced view, without your 'rose-tinted' glasses!

It could be that you simply do a 'pros and cons' checklist to understand all of the positive and potentially negative implications of going ahead with any idea, initiative or action.

Moving in the right circles

There is a strongly held view that who you spend time with is who you become, and that your network is your net worth! Ultimately, if you mix regularly with entrepreneurial types and successful business owners, then some of their influences and thoughts will eventually rub off and influence your thoughts.

Conversely, if you spend time with more pessimistic people who are happy to rubbish your entrepreneurial dreams with their 'only a lucky few have success and get rich' proclamations – perhaps because they, themselves, are having a bad time of it – then this negativity will eventually rub off on you, creating doubt within your mind and inhibiting your decision making process and endeavours.

> *"You are the average of the five people you spend the most time with."*
> *(Jim Rohn)*

I met one of my business mentors Brett Akker (founder of Streetcar and LOVESPACE) at a prestigious networking event in London and also cornered best-selling author Robin Sieger (who wrote Natural Born Winners) for a lengthy chat at another London event and both have had a positive effect on my business outlook, thinking and endeavours. If you can manage your circle of influence around you, then this will have a profound effect on your own destiny.

Here are some thoughts on how you can better manage your circle of influence:

1. Assess your current circle of influence. As Jim Rohn suggests, sit down and work out which five people you spend the most time with. You may want to exclude partners and family members, but if they have an influence on your business thoughts and endeavours, keep them in. Grade them on positivity, creative thinking, shared values and vision. If they are more negative than positive, more sceptical about their and your potential success and have no real dreams or vision themselves, either stop mixing with them or spend less time with them. If any of your current circle of influence offer supportive advice that broadens your horizons, then look to spend more time with them by perhaps working more collaboratively.

2. Choose your environment carefully. As mentioned previously, networking events and seminars are a good place to start when increasing your circle of influence, but the environment must be right. If you are looking to start a business in a particular sector or have an established business within a certain market, then you should be going to events, exhibitions, conferences and seminars that relate to that sector or market. Do not discount any non-sector related events, as often you can pick up new contacts and new thinking at any type of event – but be choosy, as there is only so much time in the day to network (along with everything else that must be done within a fledgling business).

3. Identify potential influencers for your circle. Look for more positive role models, potential mentors and influencers at local, regional or national business support groups, sector related associations and institutes, networking events, workshops, seminars or mastermind groups – then get properly acquainted. Once you have earned a place in their circle, then feed into their positivity and shared visions. Also, explore their contacts to see who inspires and influences them, as these contacts could have a major influence on you.

4. Grow your circle of influence organically. The key to having a strong, supportive and effective circle of influence is to be selective but also to not appear to be too desperate or sycophantic, as this will make most potential influencers give you a wide berth! Start off with local friends, business associates and acquaintances that are not complete strangers. I like to arrange what I call a 'chattaccino' with my contacts – an informal discussion over a cup of good coffee – as this is a good way to explore any shared interests or common ground. Move on to a lunch meeting or alternatively invite them to a business event that you might be attending. Another way is to offer to interview them or do a feature on them for a social media post or podcast. Once you are part of their circle, then ask them to broker an introduction to anyone else in their circle that you have identified as potentially being an ideal influencer for you. Be subtle with this approach as you do not want to appear to be just using them to get your next contact.

5. Improve your own influencing skills. If you want to add a worthy influencer to your circle and become part of their circle, you first have to build enough rapport to demonstrate any shared values and what your worth is. There are many classic best-selling self-help books, such as Dale Carnegie's How to Win Friends and Influence People or Stephen Covey's The 7 Habits of Highly Effective People, that can help you build sufficient rapport to influence others, but all you need to remember is to treat people as you would like to be treated. Actively listen (rather than passively listen) to really understand someone when conversing and remember to smile, as this demonstrates warmth. Be sincere and genuine with your interest and use their name in the conversation, as this builds familiarity. Communication is generally recognised as being 55 per cent body language, 38 per cent tone of voice and 7 per cent spoken words – so be mindful of your demeanour and mood.

Mind and body in harmony

The terms wellness and wellbeing are now well established and most people will have a general understanding of what the terms mean, but for those that are unfamiliar with how they differ, the two separate definitions are:

1. Wellness – referring to your overall physical health
2. Wellbeing – referring to a more holistic, whole-life experience of feeling good

It's really important to make sure that both your mental wellbeing and physical wellness states are in good order because they need to work in harmony for you to function at an optimum level.

When mind and body are optimised, you as a person will stand more of a chance of realising your true full potential.

I have previously gone into a lot of detail about the mental approach to business ownership and developing your entrepreneurial sales mindset, but your physical state is just as important, because if your body isn't functioning properly, then your brain (and your mind) will not be able to function properly either.

> *"Happiness is when what you THINK, what you SAY*
> *and what you DO are in HARMONY."*
> *(Mahatma Gandhi)*

Modern sedentary lifestyles

A normal working day for the average adult can mean a lot of time sitting at a desk and in front of computer, e.g. an inside salesperson, or perhaps sitting in a car for extended periods, e.g. a field sales representative.

A whopping 81 per cent of UK office workers spend between four and nine hours each day sitting at a desk, and this equates to an average of 67 sedentary days per person per year (according to a survey by office equipment suppliers Fellowes).

On top of this figure, 64 per cent claimed their office environment also had a negative impact on their general health.

These extended periods of immobility are not good for our posture or our general physical health. Having your workstation set up properly (with the aid of an occupational health specialist) will certainly help with your general posture, as will getting up at least once an hour to stretch and take a short walk – but these measures alone won't help with your overall general physical health.

Taking regular exercise

Taking regular aerobic exercise is essential for good physical health. Aerobic (or 'cardio') exercise is any type of cardiovascular activity which increases your heart rate and will include brisk walking, swimming, running or cycling.

For most healthy adults, the recognised recommendation for regular aerobic exercise is 150 minutes of moderate activity per week or 75 minutes of vigorous activity per week (or a combination of both types of activity).

Even a twenty-minute walk per day at a normal walking pace is beneficial for those that are desk-bound for long periods of the day – so take a walk in your lunch break and get some vitamin D at the same time, if the sun is out!

Maintaining your mental health

Maintaining your mental health is critical in business, but there is still some stigma around mental health issues (especially amongst men).

The mental health charity Mind says that one in four people will experience some form of mental illness each year, but the traditional business approach to this issue has often been 'don't bring your issues to work', with the expectation being that you just 'power through' them.

Now, through education and with the government giving mental health parity with physical health, there is more awareness around the subject matter and how you can prevent mental issues becoming much more serious and entrenched.

NHS figures show that one in five women suffer from anxiety or depression compared with one in eight men but women are more likely to seek the help they need. Anxiety can also manifest itself differently according to gender, but for men, their behaviours due to stress can be quite displaced, hence the term 'Manxiety'.

> *"We readily go to the health club when our doctor suggests we need more exercise, but we regularly neglect the 'mental health club' that our well-being more truly requires."*
> *(Pico Iyer)*

There are lots of resources to help you be more aware of mental health in the workplace and to spot the early signs of anxiety and depression.

The NHS has a Mood Assessment Quiz (for spotting the signs of stress, anxiety or depression): *https://www.nhs.uk/conditions/stress-anxiety-depression/mood-self-assessment/*, and this could be a good place to start if you have any concerns.

Mind also has some good mental health resources for the workplace: *https://www.mind.org.uk/workplace/mental-health-at-work/*

Maintaining your cognitive function

The average human body is made up of 60 per cent water, whilst our brain consists of over 70 per cent water. If we do not maintain our body's water supply by taking on plenty of fluids and we become dehydrated, our body is unable to perform its normal physical and mental functions properly.

The symptoms of dehydration include:

- feeling thirsty
- feeling dizzy or lightheaded
- feeling tired
- dry mouth, lips and eyes
- dark yellow or amber coloured pee
- peeing little, and fewer than four times a day

Tiredness, headaches, fatigue and dizziness are signs of severe dehydration, with as little as one per cent dehydration causing a negative effect on our mood, memory and general cognitive health.

Dehydration affects our levels of attention, concentration and judgement. This increases the odds of us making a rash or wrong decision – which can then have a detrimental effect on the health of our business.

Many health professionals recommend drinking two litres of water per day (or eight eight-ounce glasses per day) but other drinks such as fruit juice, milk and tea will count towards your daily intake target. Caffeine in coffee is a known source of dehydration, as is alcohol, so these should be factored in when calculating how much fluid to take on each day.

Keep a water bottle with you (especially in the warmer summer months) and take regular small sips throughout the day. If you are sweating (which is our body's natural way of cooling down) then drink extra fluids. Your pee should also be a pale clear colour (rather than vivid yellow) if you are sufficiently hydrated.

You can stay mentally alert and keep fatigue at bay by staying in good mental and physical shape. This will then help you cope better with the exertions and rigours of small business ownership and decision making.

Avoiding isolation

Being a 'solopreneur' or 'homepreneur' can be a lonely business, and often when things are not going so well, the temptation is to lock oneself away and avoid any contact with our fellow peers and business associates.

Indeed, according to some recent research by Epson (the electronics company), who quizzed 1,000 UK freelancers, 48 per cent admitted to finding it lonely and 46 per cent said it was even isolating. A further 32 per cent of those polled said they missed office banter and 29 per cent said they missed being part of a team.

Isolation has its benefits, e.g. if you need a distraction-free environment, but some people can cope with working by themselves much better than others and this is mostly down to your personality type.

Some will also see the liberation that self-employment brings as outweighing any negatives such as being on your own for large parts of the working week.

> *"If isolation tempers the strong,*
> *it is the stumbling-block of the uncertain."*
> *(Paul Cezanne)*

I, personally, never had a problem working alone and managing myself in the many home-based roles that I had as an employee and now as a self-employed business owner – but the transition at first can take some getting used to.

I am actively involved in several business support and membership groups, either as a local leader or at committee level, and these have been absolutely essential for me maintaining my sanity and having regular social human contact, outside my self-employed home office existence.

If isolation is starting to have an effect on your mental wellbeing, then consider:
- Joining a local business group (preferably where you can generate sales leads)
- Attending regular industry events (to increase your network of contacts)
- Swapping your home office for a local serviced office or co-working space
- Visiting your clients more in person (rather than telephoning or emailing them)
- Going for a walk, run or cycle at some stage of the day, e.g. lunchtime

There are many business support groups and networking events in every region across the UK. It may be trial and error to find out which groups or organisations are best suited to you and your particular needs.

I found the Institute Of Directors (for my professional network) and Enterprise Nation (for my start-up, early stage business and fellow homepreneurs network) to be best suited to me, as well as the ISM (Institute of Sales Management) for collaboration and networking with my fellow industry peers.

The trick is to spot the early warning signs of isolation – e.g. lack of motivation, low mood or even depression – and take some action fast, otherwise your mental health as well as your business health could suffer.

Other cognitive health factors

Genetic, environmental and lifestyle factors are all believed to influence our cognitive health. Some of these factors may contribute to a decline in thinking skills and the ability to perform everyday workplace tasks.

Genetic factors are passed down and cannot be controlled, but environmental and lifestyle factors can be controlled.

These controllable factors include:

- Having a balanced diet
- Exercising regularly
- Getting a good night's sleep
- Having a good work/life balance

> *"The best six doctors anywhere and no one can deny it are sunshine, water, rest, air, exercise and diet."* (Wayne Fields)

Depression and stress are other cognitive health factors that can be readily addressed. Being depressed can make it difficult to pay attention and focus (which can also affect memory) on even performing standard everyday business tasks.

Stress and anxiety will also affect your levels of concentration. When your mind is occupied with other matters, overstimulated or distracted, your ability to remember can suffer accordingly. Stress caused by an emotional trauma can also lead to issues with loss of concentration and memory.

If you are not sleeping well, finding it hard to concentrate, suffering from memory loss, feeling depressed or anxious, visit your GP in the first instance (who may want to refer you to a clinical professional) but don't ignore the warning signs, as most cognitive health conditions are easily treatable.

TOP TIP: Being more entrepreneurially minded will help you evolve your business and being more sales-focused will help you generate more consistent and predictable sales. If you are still not convinced about the concept and business case for being more entrepreneurial sales minded, then please read on further.

8. ASSESSING YOUR ENTREPRENEURIAL SALES IQ

Now that you have determined where you sit on the 'Entrepreneurial Sales Spectrum' you will need to assess your entrepreneurial sales IQ, so that you can put in place a programme to develop your entrepreneurial sales skillset.

> **"Research shows that willpower is more important than IQ. That's why the point isn't to become smarter, but to become more self-disciplined."**
> *(Adam Kirk Smith)*

You entrepreneurial sales IQ involves two basic elements:

You will need to assess both of these acumen elements independently and then align your findings so that you can put in place a plan for developing your current entrepreneurial sales IQ.

This involves testing where you are now, assessing your current skillset, understanding what type of personality you are, working out what your personal motivational factors are, identifying what resources you need to develop and then implementing an action plan.

Test > **Assess** > **Identify** > **Action**

Following this sequence and combining all of your findings will give you a blueprint for your own personal bespoke entrepreneurial sales development plan.

Testing and assessing your skills

Some aspiring (or developing) entrepreneurial sellers will be looking to build a sales team around them, whilst others will be looking to go solo.

For those that are looking to build a sales team, assessing your interpersonal skills is important. Whilst some are born naturally gifted leaders, others are not obvious leaders of people, but the skills needed to influence and lead others can be learned and improved upon.

The first thing to do is understand where you are when it comes to leadership skills and there are many resources you can use, e.g. psychometric testing, for determining what type of leader you are or could become.

Testing your entrepreneurial IQ

Forbes features an entrepreneurial quiz which is based on an original Open Forum article *(http://www.openforum.com/articles/forget-harvard-heres-the-entrepreneur-test-for-the-rest-of-us)*.

Mind Tools *(https://www.mindtools.com/)* has a number of resources for determining your leadership skillset.

Psychometric Tests *(https://www.psychometrictest.org.uk/entrepreneur-test/)* also has a '50 Item Entrepreneurial Questionnaire Test' but there are lots of online tools for determining your entrepreneurial and leadership skills, many of which are free!

When you know where you are with your entrepreneurial leadership and business skills, you can then think about developing your skills. Again, there are numerous resources for this; you can access remote online learning courses through many business schools and educational establishments.

Entrepreneurial learning resources

One of the oldest business schools here in the UK is the Cranfield School of Management *(https://www.cranfield.ac.uk/som)*, which does MBA programmes in entrepreneurship. Other educational establishments offer Diploma, BA and MSc Entrepreneurship courses (see 'Learning Systems', page 104).

Understanding your entrepreneurial leadership skills is only half the story. You will also need to understand where you are with your current level of sales acumen.

Testing your sales IQ

Your sales aptitude or ability to sell can be measured over a number of fronts. Sales ability isn't just about experience and expertise, it's also about your people skills, personality type, motivation and attitude.

The key to entrepreneurial sales success is for you to dedicate yourself to continuous improvement. Daily or weekly incremental improvements motivated by using micro-resolutions (immediate short-term goals) will help you become bigger and better than the sum of your parts. Always be curious and don't stop learning, as this is how we all improve!

Determining your personality type

Successful salespeople are normally driven self-starters. Their drive isn't always overt, i.e. obvious to everyone, but they are typically enthusiastic, willing to seize opportunities and driven – not giving up when others might 'call it a day' sooner.

A good example of this is that, according to the National Sales Executive Association, 80 per cent of sales are made on the fifth contact, yet 48 per cent of salespeople do not follow after the first contact, e.g. after sending a proposal, and only 10 per cent make more than three contacts.

Successful salespeople are normally good communicators, so get on with all types of people. They are also, typically, active listeners, so really understand others' situations, and they are effective negotiators too – but not always dominant outgoing types.

Approximately a third of the population are introverts, a further third extroverts and the final third ambiverts (a combination of introvert and extrovert), but studies show that extroverts are not normally the most effective sellers.

According to the eminent psychologist Terrence Watts and his evolutionary psychology model 'Warriors, Settlers & Nomads', the Warrior (a tenacious, determined type who needs to be in control) typically ends up in senior management roles, the Nomad (a charismatic, evidential type that gets restless and needs constant stimulation) typically ends up in sales roles and the Settler (a sociable, intuitive, adaptable type that possesses a need to be liked) naturally migrates towards care, HR and education type roles. Settlers, however, often transition successfully to customer service, account management or business development-type selling roles.

I've already spoken about extroverts, introverts and ambiverts, and whilst it can be an advantage to be an 'outgoing' type of person in some selling situations, e.g. a nomad, it isn't a prerequisite for being in sales in general.

Some of the most effective salespeople I've worked with were quiet, considered and thoughtful types that didn't crave the limelight, i.e. introverted settlers, yet they achieved consistent sales results.

Whilst you can't really change your intrinsic personality, you can be aware of what your type is and therefore able to make some allowances and adjustments when dealing with other types of personality.

Personality trait testing

As referenced earlier, I favour the 'Warriors, Settlers, Nomads' personality traits model for understanding and spotting other personality types. Some people may not have a particular dominant trait (as we all possess elements of the three different traits). Maturity can also help you rein in an excessively prominent trait, whilst developing your less prominent traits, to become a more balanced rounded person.

I use this model with my clients (and their salespeople) as there are only three distinct personality traits to understand, whereas with other personality trait models, many have much more and sometimes very nuanced profiles, which make it harder to understand or spot a particular personality trait.

An archetypal Nomad seller will require additional structure and stimulus to keep them selling at an optimal level and they notoriously have a short attention span, so may need regular motivation.

What's your motivation?

The old cliché is that all salespeople are motivated only by money, and whilst financial reward is important for many salespeople, it isn't normally the only factor. Commission and bonuses can supplement a lower basic wage and help the salesperson maintain a certain standard of living, but they normally do what they do for more than just the money.

Recognition is a big motivator for some salespeople, i.e. being 'top-dog', and many sales organisations create a competitive environment that acknowledges and rewards over-performance. Other salespeople prefer the buzz of closing the deal, which can be a powerful aphrodisiac for some.

Wanting to better oneself is a motivational factor for many salespeople and this can tie in with money because betterment typically means advancement, promotion and, therefore, a pay rise.

Culture is another factor, and companies that value their salespeople, give them the tools to do their job and provide a positive learning environment tend to hold onto their salespeople longer than do those that do not provide this supportive culture.

The sales profession can be transient in nature too – 'the grass is always greener on the other side' – but Sir Richard Branson has a positive take on staff retention: 'Train your staff well enough to leave but treat them well enough to stay.' If you don't train your staff (because you fear that a competitor will benefit from your training investment at a later stage), they are going to leave anyway because of feeling undervalued!

Finally, one of the biggest motivators for me (and many others that I've sold with) is helping others. Having a greater purpose, i.e. making a real difference to someone's life, is a real motivational factor and often a sales target will look after itself, as long as you are helping as many people as you can.

Motivational strategies

Once you have pinned down what really motivates you (when it comes to sales and selling) you can base most of your future strategies and activities around this motivational lever, to help keep your momentum going.

If money is your driver, then keep a running total of your sales revenue, adjust your target accordingly and track your running total every day, to see your revenue and profits increase.

If helping others is your 'thing', then collect as many testimonials and case studies as you can and use these when times are leaner to remind yourself of your greater purpose.

If betterment is your motivational factor, draw up a PDP (Personal Development Plan) for yourself and highlight where your skills gaps are. Then schedule some appropriate coaching or training and track your development as you go. Many courses provide a completion certificate, so download these and keep a record to remind yourself of your ongoing development.

Finally, if you have a sales team, perhaps you could use gamification to creative a healthy competitive environment, whereby team members can track their own sales performance against their counterparts' and egg each other on to greater numbers.

Having the right attitude

Convincing sellers convince others because they sell with passion. If you aren't passionate about what you are selling, then how can you expect a potential buyer to be convinced as well? Having a positive attitude, communicating what you do with real passion and showing how you are able to help a buyer is, therefore, a must when it comes to sales.

Being naturally curious is also vital when it comes to successful selling. The ability to dig down deeper and understand a problem or the real meaning of something (whether that be a situation or an answer to a question) is essential.

With a prospective customer, this means really understanding what the prospect's challenges, needs and wants are, which then allows a salesperson to propose a suitable solution for resolving that prospect's problems or meeting their needs and wants, i.e. materially helping them.

Being curious also means you can broaden your outlook and knowledge, which aids self-development, betterment and advancement. Successful sellers won't necessarily feel passionate about every product or service that they sell, but having the right positive mental attitude and projecting a positive demeanour can go a long way as a substitute for less passion.

Stiffen your resolve but not your outlook

Being professional doesn't necessarily mean being cold, stuffy and humourless either. Humour and levity (in the right place and at the right level) can be a powerful selling tool for putting a buyer at ease and helping to build rapport. The best business quote I came across in relation to this, and one I try to abide by, is:

> *"Take your business seriously – but don't take yourself seriously."*
> *(Unknown)*

The ability to laugh, especially at yourself, will stand you in good stead for dealing with the ups and down of establishing and maintaining a profitable and viable small business!

Master your self-discipline

People with a higher degree of self-discipline spend less time debating about marginal things that may improve their business success. For others, they can get bogged down with the less important things that make very little difference to their business success.

It can be quite easy to get distracted by the everyday 'stuff' that all business owners have to deal with, e.g. chasing bills, IT issues and staying on top of emails and social media messages. This can divert your attentions from the bigger, more lucrative picture, e.g. working on your business, rather than always working in your business.

If you lose focus on the bigger picture because of these day-to-day lesser distractions, this can affect your longer-term business health. The next thing you know is that another season has passed you by and all those innovative plans that you had for your business have been parked for yet another season or year!

To avoid the damaging effects of IPA (Inaction, Procrastination, Apathy), there are certain things that you can do to improve your focus and willpower, which will then help you take more control of your business and personal choices:

1. **Identify your weaknesses**: Recognise your flaws and then decide if you can overcome them. Outsource if you feel that your weaknesses are insurmountable.
2. **Set clear goals:** Always understand what your goal is and then put in place a plan that outlines the steps that you need to take to achieve your intended goal.
3. **Avoid distractions**: The fewer distractions you have, the more focused you will be on accomplishing your set goals. Remove temptations and other bad influences.
4. **Work on your willpower**: Willpower is determined by your beliefs. If you believe that you can achieve something, then it is much more likely to happen.

5. **Learn from your mistakes**: Where there is failure, there is a lesson learned. Don't punish yourself over mistakes but learn from them and take some remedial actions.

6. **Be prepared**: Formulate a business continuity plan, so that you can prepare for and manage any work-related issues, that might affect your business operation.

The silent business growth killer...

I. P. A.

Inaction

Procrastination

Apathy

Image by Alexas_Fotos from Pixabay

"We are what we repeatedly do. Excellence then is not an act, but a habit."
(Aristotle)

Self-discipline is indeed a discipline, i.e. it is learned and then has to be applied consistently. Being continually focused and diligent in your daily behaviours will help you sustain your newly found self-discipline.

Sales acumen learning resources

There are numerous channels and options when it comes to choosing a learning resource to help improve your sales acumen, but you might want to start with one of my online specialist mini or full sales training courses (see my website).

Local business groups will typically run periodic sales courses, so check their training itinerary and attend business shows, where sales trainers and speakers normally offer training sessions, workshops or seminars.

Consider joining a specialist sales organisation. As a Fellow of the ISM (Institute of Sales Management), I keep up to date with the world of sales and the latest best sales practice by using their industry leading tools and resources.

The ISM provides sales qualifications (certificate level 2 to diploma level 6) in Sales & Marketing, Sales & Account Management and Strategic Sales. Anglia Ruskin University also offers an online BA sales degree course for serious sellers.

There is no substitute for experience, so once you have some sales theory, put your theory into practice by learning on the job, i.e. going out and selling. Also, look for speaking spots to help position yourself as the 'go to' authority in your sector, and remember to pitch your offering, and a special offer, to your respective audiences.

Find a sales mentor or coach or consider shadowing someone who is more experienced and proficient in sales, as this will help you see proper selling at first hand. Ask to accompany them on a sales call (which they may not agree to, but if you don't ask, you don't get) or view some online TED talks or YouTube tutorials. Alternatively, listen to a sales-based podcast, e.g. check out Scale Your Sales by Janice B Gordon.

Role play (practising what you will say to potential buyers with someone that can give you constructive feedback) can really help embed some best sales practice, and using a formulated elevator pitch (for networking), a phone script for cold calling (for generating leads), email templates (for generating or nurturing leads) and a proposal template will all help in enhancing your sales technique.

 TOP TIP: **Research online sales related resources such as Salesforce.com, HubSpot, insidesales.com, The Sales Management Association, The ISM and other platforms. Join or sign up to their articles, newsletters, webinars and special offers - to help advance your own sales know-how, acumen and knowledge.**

9. DEVELOPING YOUR ENTREPRENEURIAL SALES SKILLS

There is no substitute for learning on the job, and the most effective way to develop your entrepreneurial sales skills is to run your own business or at least test your concept with a side hustle.

Generating sales is going to be quintessential for your business, so you will need to develop your sales knowledge, know-how and intelligence – your 'Sales IQ'. Once you've developed your Sales IQ you can think about fully enabling and optimising your sales (I will be covering sales enablement later in this chapter).

For a seasoned sales professional who wants to start a business, a great way for them to test their entrepreneurial sales 'mettle' is to have a part-time or freelance project that provides a supplementary income, in other words a side hustle.

Typically, side hustles are born out of a hobby or an interest and are great proving grounds for a larger-scale business concept. A side hustle will also help you learn what skills are needed to run and maintain a viable full-time business.

Creativity

Creativity has transformed the business world from the Industrial Revolution in the late eighteenth century to the present day Fourth Industrial Revolution (4IR), which includes technologies such as artificial intelligence, quantum computing, 3D printing and the internet of things.

Creativity isn't just limited to artists and designers: anyone can create something new by building on and improving something that already exists. A good example of this would be Uber, who built on something that already existed (minicabs). They applied some creative thinking ('convenience-centric' work practices) along with modern technology (the Uber App), and that is how they created something new.

Surrounding yourself with many different influences can help with this creative thinking process. Everything that we experience is constantly re-configured in our brain: sights, sounds, smells, ideas.

These influences are combined with what's already there, i.e. existing memories and knowledge, and the result is something new. In other words, creativity is not about making something out of nothing, it's about re-fashioning things that already exist. If you want to be more creative with your business model, then look at what already exists in your sector or niche (or a new sector or niche) and see how you might improve on it!

Your library of influences

Creating a library of influences that may or may not have relevance to your current business model, sector or niche is one way to get creative. You can use Pinterest (or similar) to save interesting images that you found on the web or sign up to interesting business forums and educational sources.

Get out into the world, be curious and be observant, but don't stick to traditional influences. I attend non-industry events, view non-sector TED talks and listen to unrelated podcasts, not just for recreation but to also expand my library of influences.

Build your library of influences

Creativity can also be therapeutic and healing. An example would be stroke survivors who are encouraged to take up art, as this has been found to be more therapeutic and aid better rehabilitation compared with just conventional physical therapy alone.

Non stroke survivors could also benefit from taking up one of the arts as this can help promote wellbeing and fulfilment as well as offer a 'stress relief' valve from the daily rigours of running a small business.

Creative writing can also offer a similar release but more importantly, could help you craft more engaging and interesting posts, articles and marketing content. Even writing a book as I have done (which can help position you as an industry expert) has creative benefits, but you don't have to be a 'wordsmith', as a copyeditor will edit your work. You could even enrol on an online or local 'creating writing' course, which you can do in your own time and at your own pace.

Finally, learning a new language or musical instrument is a great way to get creative, as well as giving you new skills, ideas and perspectives. Being able to speak a new language could potentially open up new market opportunities for your business, whilst playing a new instrument may open up a new network of influencers and introducers for you and your business.

Use your 'six' thinking hats

Part of the trick with being creative is to break old habits. In his book Six Thinking Hats (created and published in 1985), Edward de Bono, MD, PhD, suggests that you can use the following exercise to move your brain outside its habitual way of solving problems.

Each coloured hat represents a different style of thinking and put together, can give you a multi-dimensional view about a problem or challenge:

White hat: Concentrate on your available data and look for past trends, whilst attempting to fill in any knowledge gaps.

Red hat: Use your own intuition and emotional response but be empathetic to how others might react.

Black hat: Take a critical view by considering all of the different ways why an idea might not work.

Yellow hat: In contrast to 'Black hat' thinking, look at the problem with a more positive eye and evaluate the benefits.

Green hat: Get crazy with your ideas and let your creative persona take over by imagining the most unusual solutions to the problem.

Blue hat: This represents logical and reasoned thinking. Employ your 'leader' persona and imagine how you would assign others to find a solution.

Using this more creative approach can help you tackle a problem from many more angles, which in turn can produce more than one solution. You can then rank your multiple solutions according to practical factors such as time, cost and resource.

Creative hacks

Use these additional creative hacks listed below to summarise how you can take your entrepreneurial sales creativity to another level:

1. Try something new – as this helps bypass your default thinking. Don't be bound by specialisation as you can still be niche in what you do but not limited by the traditional influences associated with your industry.

2. Push boundaries – as this will help you explore the range of possibilities and understand the limits of what will work and what won't. This will then allow you to pivot your business model more easily (if needed).

3. Embrace failure – because this is how we all learn. Many won't take a chance on something for fear of failure but failure itself can often spawn some of the most creative ideas.

Creativity is the most potent and transformative tool an entrepreneurial seller has at their disposal. When you are engaged with something that interests you, you learn even from failure. Don't let fear of failure trump your most creative (and potentially lucrative) ideas and try to get comfortable with feeling uncomfortable!

Imaginative thinking

We spoke about left brain and right brain thinking in Chapter 8, but it's your prefrontal cortex that allows you to imagine what doesn't yet exist.

The good news for all aspiring entrepreneurial sellers is that we are all wired for this type of thinking, but you may need to first get past some previous conditioning (being told from an early age that you are not a creative or imaginative type).

You can take your imaginative thinking to new heights by doing the following:

1. Use your imagination: This is an essential skill for establishing a distinct and viable business venture. We have already explored how the right hemisphere of the brain controls 'creativity' and this will allow you to see a gap in a market where others don't and then act to fill that gap first. Taking on something new and challenging will help you develop your creative and innovative mindset, as well as take you outside your comfort zone. This means researching new opportunities using sources such as the ONS or Statista, or signing up to one of the many MOOCs (Massive Open Online Courses) that universities release each year, as these can help you develop your understanding of a potentially lucrative new revenue generating opportunity.

2. Have a vision: This means having an aspirational understanding of what your business venture wants to achieve or accomplish in the mid to long term. Your vision can be used as a clear guide for determining your current and future courses of action. Your vision must be realistic and attainable but given the pace of modern change and the potential need to pivot your business at certain times, it should really be more for the mid-term and reviewed at regular intervals. Your vision can be distilled into a vision statement, which can then be used to remind yourself of your intended destination when you inevitably encounter those more difficult times.

3. Launch a venture: This can be daunting for those that have always been an employee. As stated earlier, a great way to start is to have a 'side hustle', which allows you to trade with the safety blanket of your main income behind you. You could also volunteer to help on the committee of a local charity or community project, as this will open your eyes to the sort of commercial challenges that they face day to day. Either option would be a good introduction for developing your entrepreneurial sales skills and gaining some practical commercial experience. It would also be a great way to engage your creativity, especially with a charity, as charities are always looking for innovative ways to raise funds.

4. Know your numbers: Your accountant, bookkeeper or relationship manager at the local bank will tell you that you need to 'know your numbers'. This means understanding your top and bottom line, i.e. sales, cash flow, net income, profit and loss, price points, gross margin and total inventory. When it comes to your sales numbers, the basic ones to understand first are average deal size, win rate and opportunities created per week or month. Modern cloud-based accounting software – e.g. Xero, FreshBooks, Quick Books, FreeAgent or Sage One – will allow you to track your financial numbers in real time whilst a CRM (Client Relationship Management) cloud-based tool such as Zoho, HubSpot, Pipedrive or Salesforce can help your manage your pipeline of sales opportunities and **track your critical sales-based KPIs.**

5. Market your message: Marketing is an essential tool for any business (including early stage entrepreneurial sellers) and is one of the best ways to define a distinct image in the minds of consumers. This is crucial for an early stage player competing against more established, better resourced competitors. By definition, small companies are more flexible and agile compared with their major competitors, so can play to their more flexible, agile traits. You can use a toolkit of modern, unorthodox but accessible marketing practices – e.g. viral videos, Tweets, Facebook pages and email marketing – to help gain a foothold in an already competitive market or make a splash in a new market. This type of marketing is typically innovative, risk taking, fast and proactive, whilst emphasising uniqueness and customer value. Focusing on innovative products and services or five-star customer service is another way to stand out from larger more established rivals.

6. Enable your sales: Sales enablement is the process of providing yourself (or the people that sell for you) with the information, content and tools to sell more effectively. Sales enablement is essential for successfully engaging the buyer throughout the buying process, whilst automating this process brings more consistency to your sales. For an entrepreneurial seller, this first means having a strategy (sales plan with a known target), using a sales process (each step of the sales mapped out) and applying some selling technique (a sales method for the key steps of the sale). Automation plays a major role with sales enablement and a cloud-based platform such as a CRM (Client Relationship Management) tool synced to your email client platform, e.g. Outlook, and email marketing tool, e.g. Mailchimp, will help with automating and enabling your sales function. Sales proposal tools are also available to help make your sales proposals and quotes look more professional.

7. Optimise your sales: This means fine-tuning how you sell once you have the basic sales enablement measures in place. It also means putting in place a system whereby you can bring more consistency to your sales (the next two chapters cover this in greater detail). Start by making sure that your marketing and your sales are aligned and that your sales process (the steps of the sale) is fit for purpose. Update your sales process as your customers' preferences change. Use KPIs for all the key selling stages (you can't improve something unless you are measuring it). Try and determine where any leaks are in your sales funnel (where prospects are dropping out) and keep your sales pipeline (active deals) ticking over by getting rid of any dead wood (opportunities that have been there for many months but not progressed). Increase your activity levels if you are not topping up your sales pipeline quickly enough to replace the dead wood. Optimise yourself by developing your sales acumen and IQ (see next section).

8. Keep learning: This ties in with having a growth mindset and always looking to expand your business knowledge and sales acumen. I am a Fellow of the Institute of Sales Management and this is an important resource for me to keep up to speed with the latest developments and practices in sales. Look to coaches or mentors with real-world sales experience, who can offer you practical hands-on help. Entrepreneurial sellers also need to keep themselves appraised of the latest buying trends and preferences of their customers, so this should mean regularly engaging in marketing and sales training. You can normally book onto a local workshop (check Eventbrite or Meetup.com) and I run regular workshops myself in London and Essex. There is also a huge choice of online training courses, but try to look for specialists, otherwise the content might be generic, not particularly detailed and out of date (check: *www.pdtsalesconsultancy. co.uk/sales-training*).

NB. See '4. Learning System' in Chapter 11 for further details.

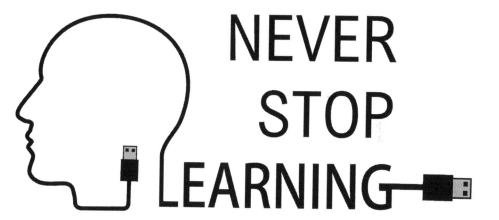

NEVER STOP LEARNING

TOP TIP: Understand your most favoured learning style, i.e. visual, auditory or kinaesthetic, and use the media that most suits you. Also be aware of whether you are more of a morning or evening person, i.e. whether AM or PM best suits your ability to work at peak levels and take on new learning.

10. YOUR ENTREPRENEURIAL SALES SYSTEM – PART 1

As with anything, you get more consistency, predictability and reliability with a system, and the same goes for sales. If you sell in an ad-hoc manner, then you are going to get ad-hoc results, so bringing a little order to your 'selling chaos' is the order of the day when it comes to generating more consistent and predictable sales!

Bringing more consistency to your sales

Consistent selling is key to avoiding those 'feast to famine' months which are synonymous with small businesses and which can be so disruptive for cashflow management and ongoing investment decisions.

A proven way to generate more consistent and predictable sales is to systemise how you sell, i.e. have a more structured approach with a set of repeatable actions, as this will help you improve your overall sales productivity, sales performance and rate of business growth. Build in some additional ability to change, adapt and innovate your sales system and you have an entrepreneurial sales system.

Having a more systematic approach to sales means that everyone in your organisation is selling the same way, including new additions to your sales team. Sometimes salespeople have to be de-trained first (to remove any bad selling habits) and a sales system will help with this de-training and re-training process, as well as giving your customers more continuity when being sold to.

The dictionary definition of a system is:

> *'A set of things working together as parts of a mechanism'* or
> *'An interconnecting network or set of principles or procedures according to which something is done; an organised scheme or method'*

Basic components for your system should include a sales strategy, a sales process, some proven selling technique, i.e. a sales method (or methods), and a database tool, e.g. CRM (Client Relationship Management) platform, with the addition of several further components.

1. **Strategy**: A formal documented sales plan with set goals and a target/quota.
2. **Process/Methods**: A defined set of steps for managing the sales cycle or one or more steps of the sales cycle.
3. **Sales Capital**: The personnel that make up your inside sales or field sales team (includes sales support and customer service).
4. **Learning System**: Your sales team learning and development tools and resources.
5. **Sales Enablement Technology**: Hardware and software that supports your sales team, sales administration and customer service e.g. a CRM tool.
6. **Review Mechanism**: A means of reviewing the performance of each component of your sales system.
7. **Sales Playbook**: A central place, dedicated manual, shared file which documents all sales (and marketing) related policies, procedures and resources.

Entrepreneurial sales system components overview:

Sales system component details

1. Strategy

Having a documented sales plan is proven to be one of the most effective sales performance optimisation measures that you can use for your business (according to past CSO Insights annual surveys).

Your business plan may well have a sales section in it, but most small business owners put their business plan to the back of a draw and forget about it once their business is up and running. A good number of small business owners may also have a marketing plan, but this will typically only cover the 'Pre-sale' part of selling, i.e. the marketing activities prior to the sale. A sales plan can therefore be used for your entire business, your sales team, a salesperson or specific sales campaign and to cover all three stages of the sale, i.e. 1. Pre-sale, 2. Sale, 3. After-sale.

According to HubSpot, the definition of a sales plan is:

'A sales plan lays out your objectives, high-level tactics, target audience, and potential obstacles. It's like a traditional business plan but focuses specifically on your sales strategy. A business plan lays out your goals – a sales plan describes exactly how you'll make those happen.'

Your sales plan should also include information about your target market, the competition, your market conditions, your sales target (or goal), your sales team structure and the resources they (or you) will need, your budget and key KPIs (Key Performance Indicators) that will be used to measure your progress and results.

The template I use for my clients also includes a value proposition statement and the mix of marketing channels to be used, so is more a sales and marketing plan.

2. Process & Methods

A sales process is a defined and repeatable set of steps for managing the sales cycle, whilst a sales method is typically a mini process for one specific step of the sales process.

| 1. Prospect | 2. Connect | 3. Research | 4. Present | 5. Close |

1. **Prospect**: Sourcing new leads to sell to. Prospecting may involve online research to find good quality sales leads, working an existing database of contacts or utilising offline sources such as networking events and exhibitions.
2. **Connect**: Engagement with early stage leads to gather information and qualify their worthiness for progressing.
3. **Research**: Learning more about a prospect as they progress through the sales process in order to offer them a more tailored experience and improve the likelihood of you closing out a deal.
4. **Present**: Typically, to show a formal presentation or demonstration of what is being sold. This stage can be involved, so typically comes deeper into the sales process and should only be for fully qualified prospects.
5. **Close**: Refers to any late stage activities that occur as the deal approaches closing. Closing varies widely but may include delivering a quote or proposal, negotiation, handling objections, getting a definitive decision, and other actions.

Steps for mapping your sales process:

Before you start mapping your sales process, you will need to determine who is involved, e.g. do you outsource your lead generation to a telemarketing company, or do you use external agents to nurture and close your deals?

Once you have determined functions and roles, then you can use a number of tools to map your process. The template that I use for my clients expands to nine steps (with KPI measures for the crucial steps).

You can use Microsoft PowerPoint, SmartArt in Microsoft Word or any other of a host of paid and free online programmes available for you to use. Your CRM platform may also include a feature where you can map your entire sales process.

Lead Generation: Understand and document your lead generation sources (both inbound and outbound).

Sales Team Structure: Document the hierarchy for your sales team and their specific roles – sales administration, business development etc.

Sales Development: Understand the buying cycle for your target market customers and the cadence (modes, mix and frequency of channels to nurture and convert leads) that your reps use, e.g. email, phone.

Customer Success (proactive customer service): Document who handles the handover for a new contract, i.e. cementing the deal, bedding in the account and conducting reviews, e.g. who will send them a welcome pack on signing?

Measure your crucial KPIs: Document how many leads you are generating, qualifying, converting and the customers you are retaining and up selling/cross-selling. Have a minimum SLA (Service Level Agreement) for responding to new leads e.g. 30 minutes for inside sales and 2 hours for field sales.

> *"30 to 50% of sales goes to the vendor who responds first."*
> *(Insidesales.com)*

Things to remember when mapping your sales process:

Remember to audit your customer's journey periodically, so you can refresh and update your 'real' sales process (rather than document your ideal 'aspirational' sales process).

Don't over-elaborate on your process but keep it simple and easy to comprehend, whilst not losing sight of your bigger picture and mission (your sales process should align with this).

3. Sales Capital

This is the structure and hierarchy of your sales team and all the personnel within your organisation that support sales.

The structure of your sales team should ensure an efficient workflow for your sales department. If set up correctly, it should also help cut operational costs and optimise your customer acquisition costs (an important metric for controlling your marketing costs).

> *Customer Acquisition Cost (CAC) is the cost associated in getting a customer to buy your product or service. These costs can include expenses for advertising, PR, content production and audience research.*

Sales drive the bottom line, so it is critical that you understand who takes what responsibilities and what part each staff member plays in supporting sales.

Every single staff member in your business who interacts with a prospect or existing customer should consider themselves to be in 'sales' – whether they answer the phone, make a delivery or interact with your prospects or customers in any other way.

Everyone else in your business should be supporting your salespeople and your sales function. There sometimes exists an 'us and them' culture between sales and operations (especially in a larger organisation) but any 'siloed' approach needs to be eradicated. Each department or business function needs to understand what part they play in supporting sales – but sales also needs to be appreciative of the support that they get from each department.

Put sales at the centre of your business...

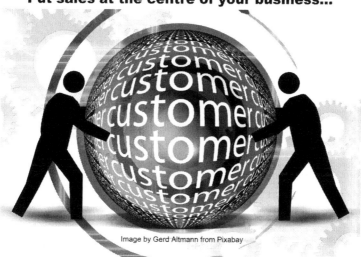

Image by Gerd Altmann from Pixabay

and put customers at the centre of your sales!

Your business needs to schedule at least a quarterly interdepartmental meeting (led by sales), so that everyone's expectations are met as to what part they play in hitting the company's next quarterly sales target and longer goals.

The traditional sales function structure

Traditionally, many small businesses have seven distinct roles that determine their sales function and support the sales team directly and these are:

Recruitment: Sales reps (representatives) are typically recruited directly by an internal HR (Human Resources) employee or by using an outsourced specialist recruitment agency (which gets paid a commission for finding and placing the right candidate). Many small companies are now dispensing with an internal HR (which has morphed into 'Human Capital') resource and instead using job sites or social media platforms like LinkedIn, to save on recruitment costs.

Marketing: Most small businesses either outsource their marketing and lead generation or use social media platforms such as Facebook and scheduling tools like Hootsuite. SEO (Search Engine Optimisation) and PPC (Pay-Per-Click), i.e. online advertising where advertisers pay each time a user clicks on one of their online ads, are other popular online methods for generating leads.

Sales Admin: This role is normally found in larger organisations, where administrative assistants support the sales teams by handling admin tasks such as customer research, appointing, CRM data entry and proposal writing. However, for smaller businesses, sales reps typically handle these administrative tasks. This may include the finance department doing credit checks on prospects (or 'sales prevention' as we use to unkindly call them in one organisation that I worked for).

Account Managers: The account manager will typically service a new account won by sales and be tasked with retaining that account and identifying upsell/cross-sell opportunities. There is often a 'handover' period between sales and account management where the sales rep relinquishes all responsibilities and commission opportunities, but these roles are increasingly being combined under the umbrella of 'business development' (see below).

Customer Service: These team members handle the day-to-day customer relationship (normally at an operational level) and will support the account manager. They are responsible for customer support (reactive query resolution) and customer success (proactive activities). Some small businesses outsource elements of this to a virtual P.A. (Personal Assistant), e.g. answering telephone enquiries when a company representative is not available.

Manager/Trainers: For many small businesses, the sales manager or sales director will have overall control of the sales team structure but also undertake day-to-day training and coaching (where necessary) or outsource periodic training to external trainers (like myself). The sales management structure can include a tier of sales managers and area sales managers who are answerable to a sales director, but for most small businesses, there is only one sales manager or sales director. Some small business owners will also outsource the sales management function to a contractor (like myself) on a retained basis to save ongoing costs.

Sales Reps: Sales reps (representatives) are responsible for selling your products and services to customers. They will work with a customer to find out what their needs are, create solutions and close the sale. Commission is normally paid if the rep meets or exceeds their specified sales target (quota). They are also normally tasked with finding new sales leads and representing their company at corporate and external events.

However you structure your sales function, make sure that everyone within it has a defined role and knows how they support front-line salespeople.

Sales or business development?

The roles of new sales and account management have historically been separated out between 'hunters' (sales reps) and 'farmers' (account managers), because each role requires a distinct set of skills and potentially different type of personality.

Now, many small businesses employ a hybrid 'business development' role which involves elements of generating and nurturing leads as well as traditional account management tasks, i.e. retaining a client account and growing that account's spend.

Modern sales requires a salesperson to have a far greater breadth of skills, but most people will have a natural leaning towards either new sales or account management. As a business owner, you may therefore want to separate these two roles out and employ specialists with the requisite skills and strengths (if your budget allows).

Business development roles can be tiered depending on the person's experience. Typically, a less experienced person would be given the title 'Business Development Executive'(BDE), whilst a more experienced person would be given the title 'Business Development Manager' (BDM).

Highly experienced BDMs are typically referred to as 'Senior Business Development Managers', with the next step on the promotional ladder being either 'National Sales' (if appropriate to the coverage of your organisation) or Sales Manager (followed by Sales or Business Development Director).

NB. I would expect any BDE to hit at least two consecutive annual sales quotas or targets before being considered for promotion to a BDM role.

Natural Business Development Progression:

Inside sales or field sales?

Most of my early sales roles were field-based, i.e. servicing a defined geographical territory whilst visiting prospects within that territory (or sitting in traffic!). I was typically home-based for these roles, so spent very little time in the office.

This role would typically entail one office-based day per week, making appointments and doing basic admin, whilst for the other four days of the week a company car (or car allowance) was provided for travelling to and from prospect appointments and sales meetings.

Benefits of field sales

1. More personal – as you can use more interpersonal skills and onsite observation when face to face and at the prospect's own premises.

2. **Deeper fact-finds** – as you can have deeper conversations with more comprehensive intelligence gathering when at a face-to-face meeting.

3. **Uncover more local leads** – as being field-based means you can call in on immediate neighbours (door knocking) and you are more aware of who is moving in and out of your local territory.

4. **Less dedicated office space needed** – as the sales team are field-based and more transient, so do not need dedicated desks or parking space (they can share a 'hot-desk' area or use a visitor parking space when needed).

With the advances in technology and connectivity such as 5G, high speed broadband, video conferencing, webinars and online demos, many businesses are now switching to an inside sales (remote selling) model, whereby reps spend most of their time office-bound (or home office-bound), generating, nurturing and converting leads, and very little time customer facing (so do not need a company car).

The final step of the sale – the close – may require a face-to-face meeting, but many businesses are also doing this final step online through video conferencing, email links and electronic signatures.

Benefits of inside sales

1. **Improved Productivity** – with less time travelling, parking and sitting in traffic jams etc. and more time spent on generating and nurturing leads.

2. **Improved collaboration** – with fellow sales team members, other office-based support staff, suppliers or management.

3. **Reduces buying cycle** – as being office-based can mean being more responsive to the client's changing needs and being more proactive, i.e. customer success.

4. **Reduced costs** – as no company car (with the associated costs of insurance, maintenance etc.) or car allowance is needed. Any field visits/customer premise meetings can be expensed at the end of the month.

Which sales model is best?

According to a MIT study, inside sales is growing fifteen times faster than field (or outside) sales and that the customer acquisition costs for inside sales are 40 to 90 per cent less than field salespeople (Source: Harvard Business Review).

Whilst complex proposals and sales cycles will always need the attributes of outside sales, many companies are choosing to switch to inside sales for the overall productivity gains and comparative cost reductions.

Most businesses would agree that a face-to-face interaction can add value to a transaction, but is this sufficient to cover the costs of sending a rep out, who may or may not close the deal? This huge growth swing towards insides sales may suggest that the answer to this question is probably no.

Other sales generating channels

The standard inside or field-based sales team model is not your only option for generating sales. Sales agents, wholesalers, re-sellers and sales distributors such as a franchise model are other effective channels for selling your products or services.

Alternative Sales Generating Channels

1. Sales Agents: External outsourced agents, wholesalers, re-sellers and other kinds of sales distributors can give you immediate access to your target market without the need to build a sales team. They can also be useful if you are trying to break into a new market, e.g. overseas, where you don't have a presence or the experience. Some Virtual Assistants will also be able to undertake elements of your sales, e.g. appointing, email campaigns and follow up communications.

2. Franchise Model: You can set up a franchise model whereby you (the franchisor) license your know-how, procedures, intellectual property, use of your brand and the right to sell branded products and services to a network of re-sellers (franchisees). This would normally require an investment from the franchisee and in return they would also get a defined operating territory. The franchisee then pays a monthly management fee in return for support from the franchisor.

3. Commissioned Referrals: You may also want to set up a referral network, to get existing customers, business associates, strategic partners, suppliers or other stakeholders to provide you with a steady supply of new customer referrals. This is normally in exchange for a commission payment or 'finder's fee' which is payable for the initial introduction or when the customer has started trading with you. The fee will be determined by how profitable the referral is.

TOP TIP: When deciding which sales channels to use, first look at the ones that your competitors and market leaders in your sector most favour. If going down the commissioned referral fees route, you can typically expect to pay 5% to 10% of the value of the transaction or the value of the first year's revenue.

11. YOUR ENTREPRENEURIAL SALES SYSTEM – PART 2

In the previous section, I spoke about how to put in place an entrepreneurial sales system that will bring more consistency to your sales, with the first three of these system components being:

1. Strategy
2. Process & Methods
3. Sales Capital

This chapter covers the final four components of your entrepreneurial sales system, which are:

4. Learning System
5. Sales Enablement Technology
6. Review Mechanism
7. Sales Playbook

4. Learning System

A learning system is essentially a collection of resources that are 'brought together' to create an environment that will facilitate various types of learning and development.

These resources can include using internal or external sources, encouraging the trainee to take on self-study learning and utilising onsite or offsite learning delivery options:

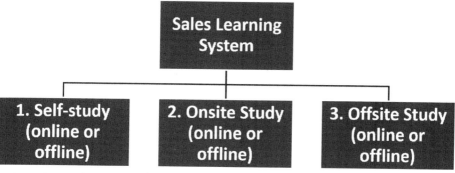

Learning systems can take a variety of different forms, e.g. online (e-Learning) or offline learning provided by the employer and at the employer's company premises (onsite), or provided by the employer at an external location, away from the business (offsite).

Employees can also be encouraged to take on their own self-study learning which would be either at their own home (outside working hours) or at an external location, e.g. adult education college, conference centre or training facility.

1. Self-study learning: The technical term for a self-taught person is an 'Autodidact' and the term autodidacticism has become far more prevalent with the huge growth in online learning platforms. Online learning options can include:

- **MOOCs** (Massive Open Online Courses) – university courses from FutureLearn
- **Dedicated Training platforms** e.g. Groupon, Centre of Excellence etc.
- **Membership organisation resources** e.g. Enterprise Nation, IOD
- **Professional body resources** e.g. industry associations and institutes
- **Conferences and seminars** e.g. The Business Show, The Sales Innovation Expo

> *"Formal education will make you a living;*
> *self-education will make you a fortune."*
> *(Jim Rohn)*

2. Onsite study: There are many benefits for training yourself and your staff onsite but the top five of these benefits are:
- **Location** – onsite training increases productivity, as staff do not have to travel
- **Flexibility** – you can make last-minute changes to the content and timings easily
- **Privacy** – you don't have to share with others, so can train on 'sensitive' issues
- **Control** – you are in complete control of all elements of the training and delivery
- **Cost** – you don't have to worry about booking an external venue or travel costs

3. Offsite study: There are fewer benefits for training your staff or yourself offsite but the top four of these benefits are:
- **Less distraction** – training away from the office avoids 'day-to-day' distractions
- **Team bonding** – offsite training helps a team to bond away from the workplace
- **Specialist facilities** – external venues can offer more space/up-to-date technology
- **Employee satisfaction** – staff feel more valued if they receive quality training

Ultimately time, budget and logistics will determine whether onsite or offsite study and learning is more appropriate for you and your set of circumstances, but don't leave it and neglect developing yourself or your staff.

> *"For the best return on your money, pour your purse into your head."*
> *(Benjamin Franklin)*

Self-directed learning

This is where an employee will provide the training but empower the employee to make the decisions for their own learning. This is achieved by transferring the onus to the learner (rather than the instructor/teacher) who themselves then decide what resources, structure, pace and delivery style are to be used.

Outcome-focused learning

Most learning systems will provide various types of learning resources with the aim of achieving a particular learning outcome (or outcomes) for the trainee.

They will also embed various strategies for assessing the levels and quality of the achievement of the trainees, i.e. have they taken on and applied their learning?

LMS (Learning Management System)

An LMS is a software application for the administration, documentation, tracking, reporting and delivery of educational courses, training programmes, or learning and development programmes.

The learning management system concept emerged directly from e-Learning and is delivered primarily via cloud-based platform providers. The main benefits of an LMS are:

- **You can train 'on the go'** – from any web-enabled device
- **Leverage social learning** – by capturing user-generated knowledge, validating it through peer review and sharing it across teams
- **Collaboration** – you can engage and collaborate with associates and partners

Personal development plan

If you don't have an LMS (which can record and track training and development) or HR programme with a similar function, put in place a PDP (Personal Development Plan) for yourself and each of your staff members (if relevant).

A PDP is an action plan based on goal setting and planning for personal development within the context of a career, education or for self-improvement.

It will also involve elements of reflection and should include input from both the employee and their immediate line manager, e.g. sales manager or director, as well as be reviewed at least annually or after the employee has had a reasonable amount of time to apply their learning (get a business associate, coach or mentor to review your PDP, if you are a solopreneur).

The process for formulating a PDP is as follows:

1. Set Development Goals	2. Establish Development Needs	3. Identify Development Opportunities	4. Formulate Development Plan	5. Undertake Development Actions	6. Record, Review, Re-set

1. **Set Development Goals**: This is about establishing the purpose of why you want to develop, i.e. the bigger picture and what you want to happen.
2. **Establish Development Needs**: This is about understanding your specific development needs and identifying the resources that will help you with this.
3. **Identify Development Opportunities**: This is about identifying which opportunities will help you develop.
4. **Formulate Development Plan**: This is about documenting what actions are needed and what timelines to adhere to for your development.
5. **Undertake Development Actions**: This is about carrying out the actions within the specified timelines, as per your development plan.
6. **Record, Review, Re-set**: This is about recording the results of your actions, reviewing those actions and re-setting your plan accordingly, i.e. evolving it.

Recommended reading
Reading regularly improves memory function by giving your brain a good workout, but it will also aid your personal growth and development.

> *"Reading is essential for those who seek to rise above the ordinary."*
> *(Jim Rohn)*

You can get most content in either hard copy or digital formats now, but it is essential to understand what your favoured learning style is, e.g. Visual, Auditory or Kinaesthetic, because an audio book may work better for you than a printed book or e-book, e.g. Kindle.

I try and read at least four business, psychology or sales related books each year and many of these come recommended by the professional bodies that I am affiliated to, e.g. Institute of Directors, Institute of Consulting, Institute of Sales Management, or by fellow professionals and business associates.

As a Times subscriber, I also have access to a list of recommended reading across different genres, but many other media organisations and forums (as well as professional bodies and associations in your particular industry) will normally feature a list of recommended reading for their members and subscribers.

Alternatively, check out the best sellers listing for your industry on Amazon, see which exhibitors are selling (or giving away) their books at industry events and business shows or view some leading TED talks on YouTube etc.

5. Sales Enablement Technology

In general terms 'sales enablement' is a term for the hardware and software that supports your sales function and team. A sales enablement technology 'stack' is a grouping of technologies that sales organisations utilise for improving their sales reps' performance and productivity.

> *"55% of top performing companies are investing in sales enablement technology to drive sales productivity."*
> *(Forbes Insights)*

The main sales enablement functions cover:

- **Content management**: For presentations, proposals and collaboration
- **Training & coaching**: For upskilling, personal development and growth
- **Analytics**: For tracking and measuring sales performance and related KPIs
- **CRM**: For prospect/customer data and sales pipeline management

Although technology plays a critical role in sales enablement, at its most basic level it also provides content, training and coaching to customer-facing employees as well as providing oversight for sales leaders and management.

6. Review Mechanism

The sales enablement technology you use should have a function for generating analytics, i.e. the ability to track and measure sales performance and KPIs, but each part of your sales system should be reviewed for its effectiveness.

To make sure that your system is properly supporting your evolving business, undertake a full sales system review at least once a year. Make sure to involve in your review all key personnel that either use or manage each of the sales system components.

A full review will allow you to identify any underlying issues in your processes and reporting measures, to find solutions for streamlining your system, making efficiency savings and productivity improvements.

KPIs, OKRs or KRAs?

KPIs (Key Performance Indicators) are typically used for one particular strategic objective, e.g. a sales target, and can help you assess your performance against that objective or target. Traditional sales related KPIs include:

1. **Leads generated** (over any given period)
2. **Leads qualified** (either by Marketing 'MQLs' or Sales 'SQLs')
3. **Qualified leads converted into sales** (customers)
4. **Customers retained** (retention rate)
5. **Customers sold more** (upsell or cross-sell)

OKRs (Objective and Key Results) are popular with larger organisations such as Google and these seek to bridge the gap between the aspirational and the realistic. An objective is identified and attached to a quantifiable target either at corporate level, department level or employee level. Typically, OKRs are reviewed more frequently than KPIs and the expectation is that not all OKRs will be met (because they usually have a more aspirational focus). If you are looking to scale your business quickly, then you may want to consider using OKRs along with specific KPIs for each of your critical business functions.

KRAs (Key Result Areas) are not a measurement but rather an internal or external strategic factor or driver for your organisation. These can be used at corporate level (tier 1) to break down your vision and goals into specific categories that will drive success, or at employee level (tier 3) to position an employee's performance and day-to-day responsibilities with the higher-level strategy of the organisation. Again, KRAs are more commonly used by large corporate entities, but could be helpful for your small business long-term vision and growth plan.

KPIs: Key Specific Targets

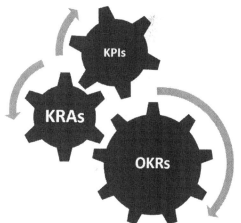

OKRs: Aspirational Targets

KRAs: Strategic Factors

7. Sales Playbook

A sales playbook is a collection of tactics or methods that characterise the roles and responsibilities of a sales team and lays out clear objectives and KPI measurements, as well as providing a common approach for closing sales. Other relevant sales related policies, procedures, processes and techniques may also be included here.

The playbook has now replaced the traditional sales manual, where all sales related information is stored in a central repository and accessed by sales management and sales team members. Administrative and user rights can be assigned to each playbook user, depending on their status and role.

Manage your playbook in the cloud, to make it accessible to your entire sales team 24/7. You can use document sharing tools such as Google Docs, Office 365, Dropbox or whatever your IT information security policy and budget dictates.

Benefits for creating and implementing a sales playbook:

- **Training new salespeople is far easier**, quicker and more consistent
- **It frees up more selling time** – as answers and guidance are readily available
- **It allows managers to capture and share best practice** amongst the sales team
- **It improves continuity and compliance** – with everyone selling the same way

Standard sales playbook categories:

1. **Company overview** (including values, vision, mission and reporting hierarchy)
2. **Sales role descriptions** (including job role responsibilities, targets and KPIs)
3. **Compensation plan** (describing salary, commission scheme or bonus structure)
4. **Value proposition** (USPs and value distilled into a value proposition statement)
5. **Products & services** (price points, specifications, case studies, testimonials)
6. **Buyer personas** (target market profiles for primary and secondary markets)
7. **Sales process** (each step of the sale – mapping your customer's journey)
8. **Sales methods** (methods for the critical steps of the sales, e.g. challenger sale)
9. **Sales cadence** (modes, means and frequency of touchpoints for nurturing leads)
10. **Messaging** (email templates, phone scripts, objection handling scripts, proposal templates, presentation decks, meeting agendas and other sales related forms)
11. **CRM manual** (help document with tips for using full functionality of your CRM)
12. **Miscellaneous** (other documentation and resources to aid the sales team)

Your sales playbook is a work in progress and should be reviewed and updated periodically as your sales process, product offering and sales team evolves.

Evolving your entrepreneurial sales system

You will need to evolve your entrepreneurial sales system to keep pace with ever-changing market conditions and your customers' changing buying preferences.

1. Design	2. Implement	3. Maintain	4. Review	5. Modify

1. **Design**: Define your sales goals, get input from all stakeholders, draw up your design and test your system. Analyse your test results, make any necessary changes.
2. **Implement**: Appoint a systems team (administrators, technical and management), train end-users and launch your system once test modifications have been applied.
3. **Maintain**: All policies, processes, training records and other time-sensitive records should be maintained regularly by an appointed technical and administrative team.
4. **Review**: Your system team should fully review your system at least annually, to make sure it remains fit for purpose and does not become obsolete.
5. **Modify**: The systems team should implement any recommended changes on a test basis and then fully integrate these changes (see previous 'Design Thinking' section).

Remember to involve all of your crucial personnel in your annual system review and ask them for suggestions on how your system can be improved (perhaps incentivise them using gamification, e.g. a competition – with recognition and rewards).

 **TOP TIP:** **Your system modifications should be based on your customers' feedback, users' feedback, what's currently happening in your operating market and what new market opportunities you have identified. Engage with your customers regularly – to keep your competitors out and keep you on their radar!**

12. APPLYING YOUR ENTREPRENEURIAL SALES SKILLS

Growing your business

Once you have developed your entrepreneurial mindset and honed your newly found sales skill, you can think about innovative ways to grow and scale your business. This can be done in three different ways:

- **Evolutionary** (Organic)
- **Revolutionary** (Radical)
- **Disruptive** (Both organic and radical)

Evolutionary innovation: Evolutionary (organic) innovation is slower and focused more on adaption rather than disruption. When innovating in an evolutionary way, the focus is on small or incremental improvements, not creating new markets.

Evolutionary innovation is the default setting for many small businesses, and what makes products valuable for customers. Kaizen (meaning continuous improvement) is another name for evolutionary innovation and typically favoured by Japanese manufacturers such as Toyota.

Revolutionary innovation: Revolutionary innovation underpins most innovation. Without these radical inventions, there would be nothing to apply evolutionary innovation to.

Revolutionary innovation, whilst radical, does not have a tangible effect on markets that already exist, neither does it create new ones. The automobile (injection-driven engines replacing horse-drawn carriages), the television and the internet are all examples of revolutionary innovation.

Disruptive innovation: Disruptive innovation combines the best of both evolutionary and revolutionary innovation because it has the unexpectedness of revolutionary innovation whilst also creating a new market.

It does this by generating new values that then overtake an already existing market. This is riskier as it can mean longer incubation periods. Additionally, disruptive innovation usually happens due to an outside influence.

All of this means that disruptive innovation is the least found type of innovation, but also one of the most contentious.

Examples of disruptive innovation are Airbnb, who provide an online marketplace for lodging, homestays or tourism experiences, and Uber, with their ride-sharing app that connects consumers who need a cab ride with drivers who are available to offer a cab ride.

> *"Every once in a while, a new technology, an old problem, and a big idea turn into an innovation."*
> *(Dean Kamen)*

Which type of innovation is right for you?

Smaller companies can be more revolutionary as they have fewer people and fewer decision makers that need to agree a new radical approach. They are more agile so can disrupt markets ahead of their larger rivals.

Larger organisations have a larger chain of command, so therefore need more people to 'buy in' to any new radical approach, and often end up innovating in a more evolutionary way. They are more risk-averse, so generally favour the safer but slower evolutionary route or they will buy out smaller more disruptive companies in order to 'acquire' their revolutionary innovation.

Ultimately, urgency, budget and speed of delivery will determine whether evolutionary, revolutionary or disruptive innovation is right for you, but cast your net wide.

Inspiration can come from any sector or industry and give you a jump on your same sector competitors. This may then lead to a lucrative acquisition offer from one of the bigger sector players!

Managing your business prudently

Managing your business prudently is key to keeping your business solvent, viable and profitable. One of the biggest challenges to any small business owner is managing cashflow and late payers.

> *"Revenue is vanity, profit is sanity, but cash is king."*
> *(Unknown)*

Cashflow is vital for any business and it is also important that you know your break-even point, i.e. when you are in profit.

The following suggestions can help you keep a handle on your cashflow and in turn keep your business-related stress levels in check:

- Track your cashflow continuously (most accounting software will support this)
- Maintain some cash reserves and an overdraft facility for emergency shortfalls
- Use minimum 30-day/60-day net terms for all your contracts, where possible
- Negotiate more favourable terms for your contractual obligations, where possible
- Offer incentives to reward customers who spend over a certain amount or to encourage them to settle invoices quicker

Late payments cost the UK economy £2.5 billion a year and are responsible for 50,000 small businesses going under each year (source: Federation of Small Businesses).

Currently, there is a voluntary code called The Payment Protection Code, which larger businesses can choose to sign up to. This code is coming under the control of the Small Business Commissioner, which should mean better enforcement and stiffer penalties for those that contravene the code in the future.

Managing your business prudently also means keeping a control of your operational day-to-day costs. There are a number of ways that you can do this and listed below are some suggestions for keeping on top of some of your larger outgoing expenses:

1. Track your costs and do a full operational analysis at least once a year
2. Automate administration tasks such as billing, accounts, payroll
3. Outsource non-essential, time-consuming tasks or processes, e.g. use a V.A.
4. Do not 'auto-renew' any business policies without testing the market rate first
5. Use a broker or comparison sites for couriers, energy and business insurance

6. Make use of discounted services through membership group subscriptions
7. Use more fuel-efficient vehicles and public transport to reduce transport costs

Insuring your business

The insurance cover you need depends on your business type. Employers' liability cover is a legal requirement for most businesses with staff. Public and product liability insurance is important if you sell products to or interact with the public, and professional indemnity insurance is recommended if your business offers advice.

If you exhibit at exhibitions and trade shows then you may well need in excess of £2 million cover for public and product liability insurance, but always check with the organiser first as it is normally a simple process to increase your level of cover.

Other types of business insurance include building and contents, cyber security, business legal protection, directors' liability, personal accident and key person insurance (recommended for partnerships). Always seek advice from an accredited insurance broker or other finance professional before proceeding with your business insurance.

Researching your customer

Some customers may ask for 30, 60 or even 90-day terms when it comes to settling your invoices. Generally, the rule is that the larger the customer, potentially the longer you will have to wait for your money.

Most large entities will have a 'Doing Business With Us' or 'Becoming a Supplier' tab on their website or you can ask for a prospective supplier pack from their purchasing department or contracts team. Many will also have CSR (Corporate Social Responsibility) commitments for treating their suppliers fairly (check their policy).

There are a few more measures that you can take when weighing up the pros and cons of taking on a new customer:

1. **Credit checks**: If your customer is a sole trader, then their personal credit rating will normally reflect their professional credit rating (an acceptable credit rating is usually 75+). Credit reports can be purchased from any of the main credit reporting agencies, such as Experian and Equifax, or you can use a comparison site such as Gocompare.com. Professional credit check agencies will normally charge more!

2. **Bank references**: Ask your prospective customer for a bank reference as this will give you a basic 'risk' summary in the opinion of the bank in question.

3. **Supplier references**: One of the best opinions you can seek is from a supplier already dealing with the customer. One issue could be that your prospective customer only asks a happy supplier to provide a reference, i.e. one they have a good relationship with. Always ask for multiple supplier references, where available.

4. **Published accounts**: Many companies produce an annual report and financial statement, which is normally found on their website. Corporate websites such as Companies House, Creditsafe and Duedil will also provide published accounts.

5. **'Pro-forma' approach**: This can help build trust by asking for immediate payment on the first few transactions. If they can pay upfront then they have

demonstrated that they have good financial health. This can work well with start-ups who may not yet be able to provide proof of their credit rating strength.

Getting paid on time

It can be a challenge taking on a larger entity that owes you money, but here are a few precautionary tips that you can take:

- Invoice them straight away – as soon as you have done the work, send the bill
- Keep on top of your accounts – be aware of when all of your invoices are due
- Work with others – such as business membership groups, consortia or unions
- Report them – check if they belong to the PPC or an industry body with a code of conduct or behaviour
- Know your legal rights – get a set of legally worded templated reminder letters
- Consider court action with a small claims online application if they ignore you

NB. Trade unions such as the GMB can now represent the self-employed and freelancers in negotiations with larger companies.

Retaining your customers

A well-known statistic is that it can cost up to five times more to attract a new customer than to retain an existing customer.

Another statistic is that just a 5 per cent increase in customer retention can increase your profits by between 25 and 95 per cent (according to research done by Frederick Reichheld of Bain & Company).

It is therefore worth your time and effort in trying to keep your existing customers, rather than having to constantly replace them with new customers.

> *"Do what you do so well that they will want to see it again and bring their friends."* (Walt Disney)

Customer retention starts with customer loyalty – so this means making your customers feel indispensable and truly valued.

If you underpromise but overdeliver (rather than the reverse) and are consistent in making your customers 'feel' special, then you can build up the sort of long-term loyalty which will survive the odd 'bump in the road' or an aggressive approach from one of your main competitors.

The main bedrock of customer loyalty is trust and this is covered in more detail in Chapter 13, but here are some practical measures that you can use to help build lasting customer loyalty and a better customer retention rate:

- Formulate a dedicated customer retention policy and loyalty programme
- Schedule periodic account calls/meetings to assess their ever-changing needs
- Identify upsell/cross-sell opportunities by using a customer spend matrix
- Be proactive with your customer service, i.e. have a customer success policy
- Personalise your service by really understanding each customer's preferences
- Ask customers for their feedback and what their perceptions of you are
- Thank them for their continued loyalty with offers, discounts and token gifts

Improving your productivity

Much has been reported about the comparatively low levels of business productivity here in the UK (in relation to our European counterparts) and this has been blamed on many factors, including lack of investment, poor adoption of technology, 'accidental' managers (who can't manage effectively) and 'zombie' companies (who are just treading water).

Some or all of these factors may be contributory to holding back the UK economy but business confidence is also a huge factor, as is strategic planning and talent retention.

> *"Productivity is never an accident. It is always the result of a commitment to excellence, intelligent planning, and focused effort."*
> *(Paul J. Meyer)*

Whilst external factors will always play a part in how productive and profitable a business is, entrepreneurs are, by their very nature, industrious types, but there are other ways of being industrious and working smarter:

1. **Set daily goals and prioritise these goals** – move onto the next goal in your priorities list once you have completed the last one, and don't procrastinate or get distracted by 'stuff'.

2. **Manage your diary more effectively** – by attributing time slots to all tasks, meetings, appointments and projects. Sync your email diaries and be a hard taskmaster with your deadlines.

3. **DOES** (Delegate, Outsource, Employ Someone) – delegate or outsource smaller less significant tasks to other internal or external parties, e.g. Virtual Assistants.

4. **Use time management tools** – there are plenty of cloud-based productivity and time management tools, e.g. apps such as ToDoist, Trello, Slack and Hootsuite.

5. **Avoid stressful situations** – stress and the resulting anxiety can have a huge impact on your productivity. Find ways to manage or prevent stressful situations. Identify which tasks and scenarios you find most stressful and work out a mitigation plan for each. De-stress by re-connecting with nature, e.g. 'forest bathing', or taking up Yoga, Pilates or Mindfulness, using apps such as Calm.

6. **Balance your work and life** – don't burn yourself out or lose sight of the things that are most important to you. Do things that you enjoy and that will help you recharge your batteries. Don't be full of regret when reflecting back on your business journey because you neglected friends, family and loved ones. Build time into your diary to attend school events, family gatherings and celebrations.

Image by
OpenClipart-
Vectors from
Pixabay

TOP TIP: Try to take regular breaks from your business. Remember to put your 'out of office' response on (you can still monitor emails periodically). Spend the first part of your break doing nothing work related. When your head is cleared, you can spend some creative time working on your business (rather than in it).

13. BUILDING YOUR ENTREPRENEURIAL SALES BRAND

Starting a business venture is exciting but also exhausting. Between building a client list, refining your sales offering, financing your operation and getting your head around all the industry related legal requirements, early stage entrepreneurial sellers barely have time to live, let alone think about how to build a distinct brand identity.

So, what exactly is a brand. Even people working in PR, marketing and advertising disagree with the definition of what a brand is!

The Dictionary definition of a 'Brand' is *'a person's perception of a product, service, experience, or organisation'*.

Other interpretations include:

> **"Your brand is what other people say about you when you're not in the room."**
> (Jeff Bezos)

or

> **"The intangible sum of a product's attributes."**
> (David Ogilvy)

Whilst this quote sums up the basic 'emotional' interpretation of a brand, a much more comprehensive definition is needed, so that you will know what elements of your business to align for a more consistent brand message.

The main practical elements of your brand would be:

- Your business name
- Your corporate colours
- Your company tagline, strapline or slogan
- Your company logo, typeface style and font size
- Your mix of products and services
- The media and communication channels you favour
- Your style and content of your blogging and social media posts
- Your personal look (style and colour of garments or uniform)
- Your company reputation

These practical elements can set the tone for your brand, but what you are really looking to do is create an emotional feeling that others can identify with and then follow.

Why is this important? Well, this feeling your brand creates will evoke certain reactions and emotions in prospective customers and your existing customers; the trick is to understand why this happens and then harness it in a positive way.

Every part of your marketing and advertising should be focused on achieving this distinct emotive feeling, and the saying 'Sell the sizzle and not the sausage [or steak]' sums up this perfectly. Some also define this feeling as your brand promise.

A brand is 'perceived'

If you were to ask most people why they identify with certain brands, they would probably find it hard to pin down. They might be able to provide a list of rational and logical reasons, but often their preference comes down to intuition or a 'gut' feeling, i.e. how does that brand really make them feel inside?

It's important to develop a brand that touches people on a more human level, because a connection based on emotion will be much stronger and more sustainable than a connection based on a more superficial 'transactional' level.

HOW DOES YOUR BRAND MAKE PEOPLE FEEL?

Image by Gino Crescoli from Pixabay

Successful brands today have emotional 'DNA' running through their corporate veins. They hold great emotional meaning for their customers, consumers or end-users and that's what makes that brand so respected, cherished and revered.

Your brand building strategy

1. **Figure out where you sit in your market**: This is about understanding your market conditions, your target market and your competitors. Research all of these elements to gauge where you are now and where you want to be in the future.
2. **Create your brand 'DNA'**: This is your distinct and emotive brand message. This should include your company values, vison, mission and value proposition, i.e. what makes you unique and why customers should buy from you and not the competition.
3. **Get internal 'brand' buy in**: Once you have your brand message, then recruit your team to this message, so they then become believers and brand ambassadors. They need to understand what your brand represents and how they feature within your brand DNA. Create an environment where your team is an integral of this message and recruit people with the same brand values.
4. **Launch your external brand 'image'**: Having decided on your company name, logo, corporate colours, slogan and other tangible assets, launch your external

brand (preferably with a media PR drive and launch party). Make sure to be consistent with your brand, e.g. always use the same formats, colours, typeface styles.

5. **Evolve your brand**: Your market, your customers and the competition don't stand still so neither should you and your brand. If your brand becomes stale or is starting to get lost amongst the competition, don't be afraid to radically evolve your brand or completely re-brand all together.

Becoming a 'trusted' brand

Trust is probably the most important brand asset you can have, as all business relationships – customers, employees, strategic partners, suppliers and other stakeholders –are based on this.

Trust should be a core value for any values-led or purpose-driven business, and it should be an integral part of your business culture, from business owner to front-line employees.

You will grow your business by growing your reputation as a trusted brand, so being ethical, honest, transparent and consistent is absolutely paramount for growth.

The 'know, like, trust' formula

Image by StockSnap from Pixabay

As consumers, we choose brands that we trust, but as business owners, we also choose employees, suppliers and investors that we trust, so it works both ways and is the universal basis for all business relationships (as well as personal relationships).

The modern connected world now allows us to get to know someone in far more detail and in less time. We are even prompted to 'like' or 'follow' those that are now on our 'radar', but there is still work to be done when converting someone else's 'like' into real trust.

The 'Know, Like, Trust' formula is used by PR specialists and marketers but can be the base for your marketing material and brand message. You can also build your value proposition around trust and this is especially true in professional services – but I will touch on this later.

> *"All things being equal, people will do business with, and refer business to, those people they know, like, and trust."*
> *(Bob Burg)*

Step 1: Establish your brand presence

You will need to build your brand presence, so that you become known as an expert or 'go to' authority in your field, as well as a reliable and trusted potential supplier.

This goes back to really 'knowing' your audience – your 'ideal' customer – and understanding what is important to them: their values, their buying motives and their preferences.

If you educate your audience about your values and these are aligned with their values, then they will be more motivated to get to know you better. If you can also demonstrate your expert credentials, e.g. through posting thought leadership pieces and giving out useful advice, then you will further demonstrate your value.

The next step for them is then deciding whether they like you enough to consider trusting you and your brand.

Step 2: Gain your audience's approval

One you have a brand presence and have educated your audience about your values, you will then need to post content that they actually want to see. This content needs to be relevant and valuable to them, otherwise they will just move on and look for someone else to like.

CTAs (Calls to Action) are important in making your audience of prospective customers take the next step in their buying journey, but aim to keep your 'sales' pitch to just one in three posts. Also, give the content that educates them and gives them insight about their world and their challenges.

We all have a natural 'self-centred' subconscious streak in us, which is known as WIIFM (What's In It For Me), and this is what we will all think when we encounter a new message, post, article or brand.

Not everyone is going to like you and your brand, so just aim for the right people, i.e. your 'ideal' client, and concentrate on getting just them to like you.

Step 3: Build trust with your audience

Building trust is all about consistency and this means being consistent with your brand message, content and behaviours. Stick with your niche, your proven marketing channels and your most effective social media platforms.

You are far better off sticking to just two or three social media platforms where your intended audience hangs out, rather than trying to do all of the platforms and be all things to all men (and women).

If you become known for being consistent in all that you do, then this will naturally attract an audience that has synergy, i.e. shared values, beliefs and outlooks.

Once your audience is more educated about you, what you stand for and what value you can provide them, then they will like you enough to now trust you.

Once they trust you, then they are far more likely to want to do business with you, but the trick is maintaining their trust, and this comes back down to being consistent!

Your trust proposition

Every small business needs to formulate a trust proposition, in order to understand the value that they provide to their customers. They then need to communicate this in a distinct and concise statement across their marketing.

Where a small business operates in a convergent market such as legal, finance or other professional services (where all operators are perceived as being alike), it is even more important to distinguish your offering on the one thing that really matters to a discerning or risk-averse buyer – trust.

This can be achieved by building your proposition around trust factors such as ethical business practice, professionalism, qualifications, certifications and experience.

Image: Gerd Altmann & Pixabay

Are you recognised as a 'trusted' brand?

Before you can implement any actions to improve your trust proposition, you will need to know how trustworthy and credible you appear to the business community at present. The best way to ascertain your current trusted status is to undertake a trust audit and you can do this by:

- Getting personal feedback from current clients (using periodic account reviews) and speaking to previous 'lost deals' about why they said no
- Using platforms like SurveyMonkey or Google Forms to get online feedback
- Doing an online audit – use search engines, social media, forums and review sites, e.g. Trustpilot – to build a log of published comments
- Using NPS (Net Promoter Score) software to benchmark against your sector rivals and demonstrate to customers that you are better than your sector average
- Looking at all of your business functions to ascertain if any part of your operation could be more quality driven, compliant, consistent and 'trustworthy'

> *"Your brand is the single most important investment*
> *you can make in your business."*
> (Steve Forbes – Forbes Magazine)

What does a TPS (Trust Proposition Statement) look like?

A TPS (Trust Proposition Statement) is a written statement featuring a compelling and tangible set of reasons why a buyer should trust you, the seller, more than the other available seller options.

A 'trusted' seller is a company or individual that is perceived as being more credible and reliable than other alternatives, so therefore less of a risk.

How to polish your trust proposition

1. **Wear your customer's shoes**: Ask for and listen to feedback from your customers and understand how your product or service plays a part in their 'bigger picture'. Use this feedback to address their perceptions, not yours!

2. **Focus on trustworthiness factors**: One of the most recognised definitions of a trust proposition is 'a collection of the most persuasive values and reasons why people should trust you and take the action you're seeking'. You don't necessarily have to be the best in everything you do, just the most trusted option in the eyes of the customer.

3. **Don't forget results**: The customer needs to feel that they can trust you but also that you will deliver on the results they seek. Use language that suggests how easy it is to trade with you and build trust through guarantees, SLAs, customer service charters etc. Reassure them how quickly you would resolve any issue that may be common to your sector, e.g. transparency around pricing or fees.

4. **Adapt your message**: You may deal with different types of customers whose buying motives are different. They may also have different worries or concerns, which could cast doubt on your trustworthiness. Use the feedback you get from different customers and adapt your trust proposition accordingly.

5. **Provide proof**: If you can't prove your claims, prospective customers are unlikely to really believe them, and your trust proposition becomes redundant. Without proof, your trust proposition will just sound like marketing speak. If they don't believe you, they won't be able to fully trust you. Have a number of credible related stories (case studies) to share about how you overcame some of your customers' initial worries and concerns and how you became their trusted partner.

6. **Be consistent with your message**: Once you have your trust proposition, adapt the message (if necessary) to all of your different marketing channels, but try and maintain continuity. You have to be clever in communicating why you are more trustworthy than others, so use believable but memorable ways to do this. Staging launch events, sponsoring other events and seeking out 'expert' speaking spots at conferences and exhibitions are potential platforms for educating the wider business community about your trustworthiness.

7. **Protect your data**: A data breach and loss of client data can harm your reputation no end. Large brands may have the budget to protect and manage any fallout from a well-publicised data breach, but smaller brands might find it harder to recover from the resulting bad press and any reputational damage (or subsequent fine from the Information Commissioner's Office).

   Basic cyber security and data protection measures should include:

   - Have an IT and cyber security policy
   - Register with the ICO (a data protection requirement for most)
   - Get accredited, e.g. ISO 27001 or Cyber Essentials
   - Understand what data you are collecting and how to protect it
   - Keep all software programs up to date
   - Use multiple authentication methods
   - Use strong passwords, change them regularly, but don't re-use them.

Aligning your operation around 'trust' factors

Your sole objective shouldn't simply be to build and earn a reputation based on trust alone, as this can be eroded in a matter of minutes.

External forces outside your control will always have a part to play in how people perceive you and your brand, but what you can control is:

- The evolution of your culture
- Your workplace practices
- Your workflows and processes

The factors above fit together like a jigsaw puzzle and can be controlled in such a way that you become an inherently trustworthy brand (which can't be eroded in just minutes).

TOP TIP: Your trust-centric culture should be ingrained and systemic, so that it exists across the whole of your organisation. Get your staff's input about improvements for your brands' standing through staff surveys, gamification etc. Also, ask other valued stakeholders for their opinion and do some competitor analysis.

14. LEAVING AN ENTREPRENEURIAL SALES LEGACY

The definition of a legacy is creating something that leaves a lasting impression or impact, but how can you, as an entrepreneurial seller, make a defined and tangible impact or do you even want to?

> **"Legacy is not leaving something for people.**
> **It's leaving something in people."**
> *(Peter Strople)*

Your legacy really starts with your own expertise and that of the people you employ. It's about starting from day one with the intention of doing good and instilling that into the values and culture of your entire business.

For me and my business, it's about giving back to society by volunteering my time with community projects that predominantly support young people and the entrepreneurial sellers of the future.

As a school mentor with an educational charity called Career Ready, I speak to year seven to eleven students about the world of work and mentor two individual students once a month at a local academy.

As a father with two young adult children myself, there is probably a parental factor in play when helping these students, but ultimately our young people will be the next generation of wealth creators and I will also benefit from the wealth that they create, in my dotage – so I guess I have a vested interest!

Creating a legacy through mentoring

I have been fortunate enough to have been mentored by a number of very successful entrepreneurs over the years (of which several I would identify as being an accomplished entrepreneurial seller). I have also mentored a number of young start-up business owners and people on customer-facing roles.

I have always been of the opinion that you should share your knowledge, especially if you have benefited from others' knowledge at some stage (it's just good karma).

Entrepreneurial sellers can leave a legacy by passing on their sales acumen, experience and know-how to others, either where the recipient is a protégé within that entrepreneurial seller's organisation or through a collaboration with an incubator start-up or any other would-be business owner who wants to be more sales-enlightened from day one of their fledgling business.

Surviving through tough trading conditions

In 2018 there were 5.7 million private sector businesses in the UK, down by 27,000 compared with 2017. This is the first year-on-year fall in the number of businesses since 2000. In 2017 there were 382,000 UK business births, again down on the previous year, in this case by 32,000. This was the biggest fall in the number of business births since 2001. By comparison, in 2009 (during the recession after the global financial crash) the number of business births fell by 31,000 (source: House of Commons Briefing Paper, December 2018).

The above statistics show that fewer would-be business owners are now taking up the challenge of starting their own business venture. For those that do start their own business, they will normally have a vision and that vision typically entails their business being ultimately successful.

Sustained success normally leads to a number of inevitable outcomes, e.g. the business owner cashes in and sells the business, they take the business global or they retire early and leave their successful business empire in the hands of the next generation (two-thirds of UK businesses are family owned).

Success, of course, is not guaranteed, and with the failure rate amongst small businesses at a disturbingly high rate of 50 per cent by year five (and this climbs to an even higher rate of 70 per cent by year ten), remaining viable and profitable is by no means a given.

This is where sales plays a crucial part. If a fledgling business is generating a good level of sales consistently, then all other factors that can inhibit that business's growth – e.g. lack of funding, bad cashflow and lack of talent retention – can be more confidently mitigated and managed.

Sustainable legacy

Being sustainably minded is also a crucial factor for establishing a solid business foundation, growing the business and then leaving a lasting legacy. With the world's population growing exponentially and set to reach 8.5 billion people by 2030, we do not know what the future landscape will look like for our own business or business community, let alone for society and the planet.

What legacy will you leave?

Image by Gerd Altmann from Pixabay

More population equals more strain on society and resources, so businesses need to be and should be involved in this life-shaping discussion.

Whilst, as businesses, we need to continue focusing on growth, profit and market share, we also need to focus on embedding sustainability into our business models, because it is the ethical and responsible thing to do for everyone concerned.

Leaving a sustainable legacy is more than just 'green PR', and if businesses set goals which drive sustainability, innovation and collaboration, then their objectives will result in real and tangible business benefits.

The sustainability business case

Customers and other stakeholders are increasingly concerned about the social and environmental impact of their purchases and according to a 2015 Nielsen report, '66% of customers are willing to pay more for products and services from companies with strong corporate responsibility programs'.

Manufacturers are now being encouraged to make things that last longer and which can be repaired, rather than discarded cheaply, and consumers and businesses alike are being encouraged to adopt the 3 Rs (Reduce, Reuse, Recycle).

Adopting a more sustainable business model can make real commercial business sense. It can help your business save costs (through adopting more environmental, time-saving and resource-saving measures) but also open up new market opportunities, e.g. with plc's, public sector organisations and the green sector.

With today's customer more sophisticated and educated than ever before, CSR and sustainability is no longer for the preserve of the large plc's – it's for all businesses. If all businesses adopt a more sustainable model, then we can all deliver real and impactful change collectively.

So, what can small businesses do in the short and longer term to drive these necessary changes?

For a business to leave a long-term legacy, sustainable actions and practices need to be implemented in the short to medium term. This has to come from the top, so there has to be a leader or a 'champion' to drive it.

Having a sustainable and socially responsible culture is crucial to attracting today's talent. Millennials (Generation Y) are predicted to make up more than 35 per cent of the global workforce by 2020 and according to a survey by Cone Communications, 64 per cent of them won't take up a job with a company that isn't socially responsible.

Furthermore, 83 per cent of millennials would show greater loyalty to a company that helped them contribute to social and environmental issues. This demonstrates that CSR is not only a good idea, but now vital to attracting new talent and securing your brand's future success.

The challenge for any business, with so many environmental, social, economic and corporate challenges to juggle, is how to strategically deliver the most value and impact.

Here are seven proven sustainable strategies to focus on that can help shape the necessary actions which are needed for building your entrepreneurial sales legacy:

1. **Be customer centric**: Focus on your customers and what value they will expect. Use this to determine what your CSR (Corporate Social Responsibility) and sustainability goals should be.

2. **Go low carbon**: You will need to measure your carbon footprint first, before you can reduce it. Be aware of what level of carbon emissions you are producing and put in place some environmental measures to reduce these.

3. **Value your talent**: Invest in training, developing and taking care of your talent. Focus on wellbeing in the workplace, which improves staff attendance, loyalty, retention, engagement, productivity and innovation.

4. **Be ethical and transparent**: Do the rights things not just when others are looking but when no one is looking. Embed this in your culture and you will then start to be known as an ethical brand that people can trust.

5. **Be authentic and credible**: Always be who you are and expect that some may not share your values. Work with those that have symmetry and don't pretend to be something you are not, otherwise you will be found out and lose all credibility (which can damage your brand).

6. **Collaborate with others**: Your reach, impact and legacy will be magnified by collaborating with others who have the same values and sustainable outlook as you. This will open up new market opportunities too.

7. **Always be better**: Adopt a culture of improvement where change is seen as 'business as usual' and a positive thing that not only helps the business to go forward but also benefits the local community.

Increasingly, business owners and leaders must consider how they can make a lasting impact that not only ensures business longevity of their brand but also creates a legacy that will contribute to a better world and the society of tomorrow.

> *"Follow your dreams and use your natural-born talents and skills to make this a better world for tomorrow."* (Paul Watson)

Being responsible

Being a responsible entrepreneurial seller means having an understanding of what impact your overall business has on the local environment and community.

The UK Parliament has recently declared a climate emergency and air quality is a huge part of this emergency, especially in cities where a recent UK 'pollution map' released by campaigners showed that 2,000 locations across England, Wales and Northern Ireland regularly exceeded recommended air quality safety levels.

As a small business, you can measure your carbon footprint to determine where your carbon emissions are coming from and then put in place a number of environmental measures to reduce your overall carbon footprint, which then helps contribute towards cleaner local air quality.

There are plenty of online carbon footprint calculators to help you measure your overall carbon footprint and these include the Carbon Trust, WWF (World Wide Fund for Nature) and Climate Care.

Larger companies can become ISO 14001 accredited for environmental management and gain 14064 (or the Greenhouse Gas Protocol) for measuring carbon footprints, but for micro-businesses or smaller, a full suite of ISO accreditations may not be practical or commercially viable.

LEPs (Local Enterprise Partnerships) or local authorities have, in the past, run local environmental management accreditation schemes for small businesses. I am STEM (Steps to Environmental Management) gold accredited through LoCASE (Low Carbon Across the South East), which is part of SELEP (South East Local Enterprise Partnership), as this free of charge; your relevant LEP may also run a similar free accredited scheme.

Even as a homepreneur, you can calculate your carbon footprint by measuring the footprint of your home, then measuring the equivalent footprint of your home office as a percentage of your overall home footprint and applying this percentage to your utility and waste bills. You will need to examine all of your utility bills (including water) and calculate the amount of travel that you take for business purposes for your final carbon footprint calculation.

Technically, as a home-based business, you should be separating your commercial waste from your domestic waste. You can employ a local confidential shredding company to collect your wastepaper (most shredded and pulped paper goes back into making recycled paper products). They will then issue you with a secure destruction certificate and waste transfer note for your records.

You can also join responsible organisations such as BITC (Business in the Community) or ORB (Organisation for Responsible Businesses) – of which I am a member – to compare and share best sustainable practice.

Image by Clker-Free-Vector-Images from Pixabay

Here are a number of measures that you can adopt from day one to ease your exit:

1. **Form a board of directors and advisers** – which will bring group accountability
2. **Communicate your progress** – using board meetings and investor updates
3. **Empower your staff** – to make decisions when you are not in the business
4. **Collaborate with others** – who could be natural future acquisition suitors

Building a culture of empowered employees could lend itself well to a potential employee buyout in the future, and employee-acquired businesses are now growing by 10 per cent or more each year.

Ultimately, building good governance in your business will increase the options for exiting your business.

Building good habits now will only help you to succeed later, whether that success be enjoying your retirement or setting up your next business venture.

Keeping your 'hand in'

When it is time to wind down and start preparing for your retirement, this can be a difficult transitional period for many entrepreneurial sellers. Hopefully, you will have enough distractions with any community or philanthropic work that you may have built up through your business ownership journey, but many entrepreneurial sellers keep their 'hand in' by sitting on advisory boards or doing several days of consultancy or project work per week.

Another way to stay active is to increase your mentoring commitments or get involved with the committee of a local business group or charity. There are plenty of volunteer roles out there if you want to fill some of your days in retirement.

Stopping work all together quickly can carry a number of risks and these include feelings of regret about not having any more real purpose in life, increased isolation and loneliness or anxiety and depression and deteriorating health because of less physical activity.

Entrepreneurial sellers, normally, will not be reliant on their state pension in retirement but the UK state age for retirement is gradually rising for men and women: it will reach 67 by 2028 and could rise to 75 by 2035.

You can check your state pension age at: *https://www.gov.uk/state-pension-age* but you can, of course, take up a private pension much earlier and start taking money from your private pension at the age of 55.

You could also use a draw down on your private pension pot to help top up your income (if still working), to enable you to work fewer hours or to retire earlier.

TOP TIP: **Seek advice from an independent financial advisor about which retirement income products are available to you. Check the Financial Conduct Agency (FCA) and government Pension Wise websites for more impartial pension information and guidance. Shop around to benchmark the level of fees that you should pay.**

15. YOUR ENTREPRENEURIAL SALES CHECKLIST

Being an entrepreneurial seller means being alive to every opportunity that comes your way, in order to generate more sales and grow your business.

This means having a wider understanding of what is happening beyond your sector, operating market and local community, so that you can create new opportunities for yourself.

With this in mind, I have compiled a seven-point checklist that you can use to build your entrepreneurial sales acumen and business model.

THE ENTREPRENEURIAL SALES CHECKLIST	REQUIRED ACTIONS
1. GROWTH MINDSET: Adopt a positive mindset about sales, wealth and growing your business; use this book to adopt a more growth-orientated mindset, as this is essential for becoming a more entrepreneurial seller. Sales is a recognised profession, so aim to sell in a professional manner and keep innovating your sales proposition. Lose any negative mindset you may still have about sales and watch your revenues, profits and business grow.	Start date:
2. GROWTH STRATEGY: Documenting a formal strategy is proven to increase the chances of realising your strategy. Write a strategic sales plan on how you intend to grow your business and generate sales throughout the year and beyond. Map your sales process, use a sales target and forecast (so you can track your performance) and identify what sales resources you need. Review your sales plan annually and whenever there is a material change to your business or your market.	Start date:
3. SALES ACTIVITY: Plan your sales activity per quarter, per month, per week and per day. Prioritise the tasks and activities that will give you the maximum return, i.e. generate the most sales. Use the 80:20 Pareto rule to understand which tasks to concentrate on – 80% of your sales revenue typically comes from 20% of your most	Start date:

4.	**PERFORMANCE ANALYSIS:** Regularly review your sales opportunities and performance. Reflect on the decisions made and outcomes taken from all of your meetings and other sales related activities. Analyse what went well and what you could have done differently. Apply your findings and conclusions to future strategies, selling situations and sales activities. Understand what 'best practice' looks like for your industry and apply this to your business model. This 'continuous improvement' approach will help your business grow faster.	Start date:
5.	**CONTINUOUS LEARNING:** Focus on extending your learning, knowledge and skills – never stop learning. Keep abreast of the latest sales practice, as well as the latest business practices, to keep your business nimble, agile and relevant. Go to sales conferences, business shows and networking events. Consider joining industry related bodies and look at sales related bodies such as the ISM (Institute of Sales Management) to keep you up to speed with the world of sales.	Start date:
6.	**SUSTAINABLE BUSINESS PRACTICE:** Managing the impact your business has is essential for being a more sustainably minded business owner. Beware of your energy usage, what waste you produce and what your carbon footprint is. Work to a code of ethics and be transparent in your financial dealings. Vet your suppliers to see how they are managing their impact and once you have gone down the low carbon route, target the green economy and other sustainable buyers, e.g. public sector.	Start date:
7.	**GENEROUS GIVING:** Generosity generates wealth (in many forms) so try and employ a mantra along the lines of 'how can I help this person' in any of the situations you find yourself in. Give advice freely and try mentoring someone who could really benefit from your experience. Get involved in local community projects or volunteer some time with a charity or non-profit organisation. This will benefit society as well as enhance your own wellbeing and life satisfaction.	Start date:

Conclusion

I started this book off by asking if entrepreneurs are born or made and whether top performing salespeople possess a natural inbuilt selling instinct.

Some people certainly do have a natural disposition towards both sales and entrepreneurship but hopefully this book has demonstrated that with the right mindset, some earnest endeavour and some thoughtful application, any aspiring or existing small business owner can become both more entrepreneurial and sales-savvy, i.e. an entrepreneurial seller (irrespective of your natural born talents).

I hope I have not come across as too prescriptive in this book; becoming an accomplished entrepreneurial seller is all about finding the right combination of business and sales related strategies, processes and techniques that are best suited to your temperament, your personality and your business vision.

By harnessing some additional entrepreneurial spirit, e.g. having faith in what you are doing and sticking with your philosophy, as well as being laser-focused on your customers and the sales that they generate for you, you will be far better equipped for the challenges of business ownership.

Your continuing journey

Your continuing entrepreneurial sales journey should be about self-development and betterment and learning from the mistakes that all business owners inevitably make along their business journey. Don't be afraid to make those mistakes either, but be more afraid of not trying something in the first place!

Others cite luck as being instrumental in whether you are successful in business or not, but I believe that there is no such thing as luck and that you make your own luck. Luck is actually when preparation meets opportunity, but you need to prepare properly to take advantage of those opportunities that will inevitably come your way.

> *"Branding demands commitment; commitment to continual re-invention; striking chords with people to stir their emotions; and commitment to imagination. It is easy to be cynical about such things, much harder to be successful."*
> (Sir Richard Branson)

Finally, constantly innovating and if necessary, pivoting your business model, is vital for building a more distinct and sustainable entrepreneurial sales brand.

This will then help your business remain more relevant and more viable in what is now a very uncertain, fast-changing and ultra-competitive marketplace.

Finally, adopting CPD (Continuous Professional Development) for your own personal growth and development and then finding someone who can benefit from you sharing your wisdom and expanded learning with them – a protégé or mentee – will help you leave behind a more meaningful and fulfilling entrepreneurial sales legacy.

Congratulations on finishing this entrepreneurial sales book and starting your journey to becoming a more accomplished entrepreneurial seller.

You may want to use this book as a pick up, put down reference guide – whenever you come across a new business or sales related challenge.

In the meantime, I wish you well in achieving your vision for business success and happy entrepreneurial selling!

Paul Durrant FISM

ADDITIONAL RESOURCES

Useful Websites

ASP (Association of Sales Professionals):
https://www.associationofprofessionalsales.com/
British Library Business & IP Centre: *https://www.bl.uk/business-and-ip-centre*
CSO Insights: *https://www.csoinsights.com/sales-performance-optimization-study/*
Enterprise Nation: *https://www.enterprisenation.com/*
Enterprise Research Centre: *https://www.enterpriseresearch.ac.uk/*
Financial Conduct Agency (FCA):
https://www.fca.org.uk/consumers/what-adviser-might-ask-you
Forbes: *https://www.forbes.com/*
Harvard Business Review: *https://hbr.org/*
HubSpot: *https://www.hubspot.com/*
Insidessales.com: *https://uk.insidesales.com/*
IOD (Institute of Directors): *https://www.iod.com/*
ISM (Institute of Sales Management): *https://www.ismprofessional.com/*
MIND: *https://www.mind.org.uk/*
MindTools: *https://www.mindtools.com/*
NASP (National Association of Sales Professionals): *https://www.nasp.com/*
ONS (Office for National Statistics): *https://www.ons.gov.uk/*
Pension Wise: *https://www.pensionwise.gov.uk/en/financial-advice*
Salesforce UK: *https://www.salesforce.com/uk/*
Sales Innovation Expo: *www.salesinnovationexpo.co.uk*
SmallBusiness.com: *https://smallbusiness.com/*
The Business Show: *https://www.greatbritishbusinessshow.co.uk/*
The Sales Association: *https://www.salesassociation.org/*

ABOUT THE AUTHOR

The author Paul Durrant is a qualified sales professional and Fellow of the Institute of Sales Management, with over 30 years' experience in sales.

Paul founded PDT Sales Consultancy in 2014 and through his lead, brings a wealth of knowledge in helping start-ups and established businesses fix their sales related problems, optimise their sales and upskill their salespeople.

In addition, Paul is an accredited EFT (Emotional Freedom Technique) or 'Tapping' coach, which is a self-administered hybrid acupressure and psychology technique for promoting physical and emotional healing.

Paul combines proven sales strategies, processes and techniques with a more holistic-minded approach to sales and business ownership.

"Many small business owners do not have a sales background, yet are typically doing the selling, especially in the early years. If this is you, then this puts you at a real disadvantage compared to your more informed 'sales-savvy' competitors. If you want to compete on more equal terms, generate more sales and grow your business faster, then it is essential that you adopt a more entrepreneurial mindset and focus more on sales. This book will help you with that."

Paul provides sales consultancy, coaching and training for business owners, sales leaders and salespeople, as well as offering cost-effective online sales training courses which range from short half-day equivalent courses to comprehensive full-day equivalent courses, all of which can be taken at any pace, over any time period.

Get a 20% discount off the online training course that accompanies this book by using the promo code EPSALES. Visit: *www.pdtsalesconsultancy.co.uk/sales-training* for more information.

Paul is also a public speaker and has spoken at many national and regional business events and venues, including The Business Show, Start Up 2019, The London Growth Hub Roadshow, City Business Library and on LBC's Business Hour phone in.

If you found this book useful, then why not leave a review to help other aspiring entrepreneurial sellers find it (please see my email address below).

To book Paul to speak at your next sales conference, seminar or event or to bulk purchase copies of this book, please email: *info@pdtsalesconsultancy.co.uk*

ACKNOWLEDGEMENTS

Thanks to my wonderful wife Heather, son Matthew, daughter Amy and wider family for their support throughout my sales career. A special thanks to my daughter Amy for her inspiration: she is herself a published author and talented creative copywriter.

Thanks also to my mentors, business associates, fellow authors and friends who contributed to this book with their comments, feedback and shared experiences, as well as to my clients for making my work so enjoyable and rewarding on a daily basis.

Printed in Poland
by Amazon Fulfillment
Poland Sp. z o.o., Wrocław

50508226R00072